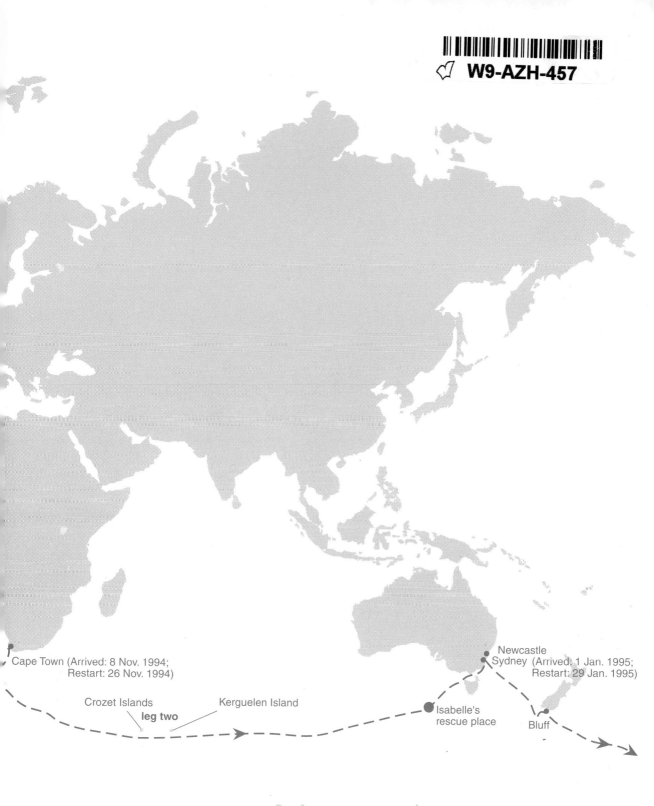

Cape Town (Arrived: 8 Nov. 1994;
Restart: 26 Nov. 1994)

Crozet Islands
leg two

Kerguelen Island

Isabelle's
rescue place

Newcastle
Sydney (Arrived: 1 Jan. 1995;
Restart: 29 Jan. 1995)

Bluff

AGAINST ALL ODDS
AROUND ALONE IN THE
BOC CHALLENGE

AGAINST ALL ODDS
AROUND ALONE IN THE
BOC CHALLENGE

ALAN NEBAUER

The McGraw-Hill Companies, Inc.

Sydney   New York   San Francisco   Auckland   Bogotá
Caracas   Lisbon   London   Madrid   Mexico City
Milan   New Delhi   San Juan   Singapore
Toronto   Kuala Lumpur

McGraw·Hill Australia

A Division of The McGraw·Hill Companies

First published in Australia by McGraw-Hill Book Company Australia Pty Limited, 1996

First published in the United States of America 1997 by International Marine, a division of The McGraw-Hill Companies.

10 9 8 7 6 5 4 3 2 1

Text © 1996 Alan Nebauer
Illustrations and design © 1996 McGraw-Hill Book Company Australia Pty Limited
Additional owners of copyright are named in on-page credits.

National Library of Australia Cataloguing-in-Publication data:
   Nebauer, Alan.
      Against all odds: around alone in the BOC challenge.

   ISBN 0 07 470331 5

   1. *Newcastle Australia* (Yacht). 2. BOC Challenge Race. 3. Yacht
   racing. 4. Sailing, single-handed. 5. Voyages around the world. I. Title.

   797.14

Cataloguing-in-Publication information for this title can be obtained from the Library of Congress.

McGraw-Hill books are available at special quantity discounts to use as premiums and sales promotions, or for use in corporate training programs. For more information, please write to the Director of Special Sales, McGraw-Hill, 4 Barcoo Street, East Roseville, NSW 2069. Or contact your local bookstore.

A video of Alan Nebauer's BOC Challenge is distributed worldwide by Film Australia, 101 Eton Road, Lindfield NSW 2070.

Questions regarding the ordering of this book in the United States should be addressed to:

   The McGraw-Hill Companies
   Customer Service Department
   P.O. Box 547
   Blacklick, OH 43004
   Retail customers: 1-800-262-4729
   Bookstores: 1-800-722-4726

Questions regarding the ordering of this book in Australia, New Zealand and South Africa should be addressed to:

McGraw-Hill Book Company Australia Pty Limited
4 Barcoo Street, Roseville NSW 2069, Australia
Publisher: John Rowe
Production editor: Carolyn Pike
Designer: Asymmetric Typography Pty Limited
Illustrator: Alan Laver
Cover photo
compilation: Steve Nebauer, A Bear Image
Cover photos: Steve Nebauer, A Bear Image; NASA Apollo Series
Cover design: Diane Booth
Typeset in 11/13.5 Stemple in Australia by Midland Typesetters Pty Ltd, Victoria
Printed in Australia by McPherson's Printing Group

For Cindy, Annie and Vance

Newcastle Australia
STEVE NEBAUER, A BEAR IMAGE

Foreword

EVERYONE has a dream. A small number of people pursue that dream and an even smaller number have the opportunity, resolve, dogged determination and personal attributes to turn the dream into reality. Alan Nebauer knew as a child that he was going to sail around the world alone. If anyone had told him then just how difficult realizing that dream would be, it would only have served to strengthen his desire and resolve.

The BOC Challenge is a 27 000 nautical mile single-handed sailing race around the world, which has been held every four years since 1982. It inspires all those who have ever contemplated a circumnavigation, be they old, young, male or female. It is a unique sporting event that enables, for example, a 70-year-old man aboard his 15-year-old 40 foot (12.2 m) yacht to compete with a 34-year-old man aboard his new 60 foot (18.2 m) yacht that has cost a million dollars to build. As the longest race on earth for an individual in any sport it is considered a race for sailors with talent and courage. There are two classes of boats. Class I consists of boats 50 to 60 feet (15.2 to 18.8 m) long. Class II consists of boats 40 to 50 feet (12.2 to 15.2 m) long. Since its inception, the boats have evolved into purpose-built machines designed only to sail fast across the world's oceans.

By their very nature, solo skippers are strong-willed individuals, all with very different reasons for pursuing such a challenging vocation. Some are natural-born sailors who regard events such as the BOC Challenge as a natural progression in a lifetime on the water. Others are committed adventurers for whom the call of the sea is a glistening lure. There are the well-sponsored professionals whose huge water-borne steeds demand great skill and nerves of steel to sail, coupled with deep corporate pockets to campaign successfully, and there are the small-budget sailors whose boats are run on a shoestring, having as many problems with their bank managers as they do with the weather.

For every one of them, sailing a yacht single-handed across oceans offers the ultimate avenue for their desire to be both mentally and physically stretched to new limits, to do something different in a world of increasing conformity and to appease an insatiable pioneering spirit. Each one makes great personal sacrifices to be on the start line, some having even sold their homes to keep their boat afloat.

Bonded by a common passion, the skippers in the BOC Challenge are inevitably brought closer still by the calms and storms, the triumphs and the tragedies that occur as the race unfolds. As Alan Nebauer describes, the disparate fleet of skippers that crosses the start line in Charleston, South Carolina, returns over eight months later as a close-knit family.

A daily inter-yacht radio hour provides, for the most part, the only regular contact with life outside your own yacht and, during the first weeks of the 1994–95 BOC Challenge, Alan Nebauer and myself formed a solid friendship. We had both put our projects together in the face of economic adversity with a lot of home-grown support as well as some corporate sponsorship, and we had both left young families ashore when we set off. It therefore seemed only right that Alan was the nearest help when my yacht hit a submerged object and started to sink in the middle of the South Atlantic Ocean. Once aboard *Newcastle Australia*, the enormity of my misfortune weighed heavily, but three weeks with the ebullient Alan was the perfect tonic for my traumatic experience. His positive outlook and natural enthusiasm not only helped greatly to revitalize my own sailing ambitions, but later in the race were to see him through his own troubled waters.

Alan's completion of the BOC Challenge ranks as one of sport's greatest achievements. All the competitors faced gear failure and breakages of varying degrees—this is, after all, a race of attrition—but each leg of the race found *Newcastle Australia* beset with problems of such magnitude that many would have conceded defeat and retired. Not Alan Nebauer. A major keel problem, electrical failure and even a dismasting were not going to stop him rounding Cape Horn and his fortitude throughout was an inspiration to all. So much so that when he arrived in Punta del Este, Uruguay, with a broken rudder he found that fellow skippers and their shore crews were preparing to build him a replacement rudder that would keep him in the race.

Back home, his course was being plotted by a Newcastle population that had taken Alan to their hearts. They listened in awe to the regular ship-to-shore interviews as he recounted rescuing myself, sailing with a jury-rigged mast and then steering with a makeshift steering system. Back at race headquarters, where I ended up working, we were equally impressed with Alan's astonishing feats of seamanship.

Alan had one of the toughest passages imaginable in what is a very tough race but at the end of it he was already talking about another project and competing in another BOC Challenge. This not only proves that we sailors are blessed with selective memories but is a testimony to his strength of character and his commitment to the task.

Although we grew up half a world apart, our love of sailing and adventure brought us together in the BOC Challenge. I hope I have the privilege of racing against him again soon. Or, if he needs a first mate before that, I'll be first in line.

JOSH HALL
Gartmore Investment Managers

Contents

———

Preface

> To be truly challenging a voyage, like life, must rest on a firm foundation of financial unrest. Otherwise you are doomed to a routine traverse.
> Sterling Hayden, *Wanderer*, Futura, London, 1979, p. 22

I HAVE never been one for routine. I had sailed over 50 000 nautical miles prior to the BOC Challenge safely and with very few dramas, mostly with my wife Cindy as companion and crew. However, my voyage in the BOC Challenge was definitely no routine traverse. Many times during the race I wished for some routine—to be sailing fast with not a care in the world—but often this was not to be the case.

To write a book about my experiences in the BOC Challenge surprizes no-one more than me. However, I was initially motivated to consider doing so by Mark Schrader, BOC race veteran and race director. Since then, many people have asked me when I am writing my story.

This book is not intended to be a complete overview of the 1994–95 BOC Challenge, nor a manual of how to do it. It is simply an account of my participation in the race and I hope that you will get a glimpse of the different facets involved in such a competition and, perhaps, glean some useful information relating to voyaging in general.

To be able to take part in the BOC Challenge is, for me, a personal achievement and the realization of a long-held goal. In all honesty, however, and I think it will become obvious as you read my account, my achievement is not one I could have made on my own. Yes, I was at sea for over eight months by myself but this was possible only because countless people believed in me and helped me to achieve my goal. This help came in the form of both monetary support, through our sponsors and supporters, and community support as friends and family contributed much in the way of time and enthusiasm for the project.

The three years of fundraising and campaigning were, in a way, much more difficult to achieve than the actual race was, though no less challenging and exciting. Cindy and I had to enter a world unfamiliar to both of us and far removed from our sailing lifestyle. We would need almost half a million dollars. With all our combined efforts we were only able to raise slightly more than half that amount. The rest we had to make up with loans and deferred payments.

At times during the campaigning, as in the actual race, it would have been reasonable to bow out gracefully for any number of reasons. However, as with anything worthwhile, there must be commitment and once we had said publicly to some of our yachting friends while cruising the west coast of Mexico in 1990 that my intention was to compete in the BOC Challenge, there was no turning back. We knew it would be hard but we had no idea of how hard it really would be.

There were many lessons to be learnt, both on and off the water. Although I am not totally satisfied with my overall place in the race, given the delays and unforeseen situations that came my way, there is much satisfaction in having completed the course.

I must extend my thanks to many people and I apologize for any omissions. I am privileged to have had the trust and support of many sponsors and supporters (see pages xv to xvii). Also, my parents, Ron and Shirley Nebauer, and family have encouraged my exploits since I was a small boy learning to sail on an inland lake. And to Cindy's parents, Max and Janiece Smith, who have always been enthusiastic about our decisions, even though they have probably lost a lot of sleep since I married their daughter and took her away to sea in early 1987.

Finally, to my wife Cindy, who has given me incredible support throughout the whole enterprize. She was the first to believe and encourage me to pursue my ambition and, frankly, it would not have been possible without her determined and wholehearted efforts that continued, without complaint, during the many occasions when our family lacked the freedom and security that comes with a regular 'nine-to-five' lifestyle.

It says in the Bible that 'where there is no dream the people perish'. I thank God for giving me the dream and for enabling me to pursue it.

Acknowledgments

I WOULD like to thank the following sponsors and supporters of *Newcastle Australia* who, with their help, made it possible for me to compete in the 1994–95 BOC Challenge.

CORPORATE SPONSORS

NIB Health Funds
NBN Television
Newcastle City Council
Brambles
Peach Advertising
Jarkan Yacht Builders

Ernst & Young
NCP Printing
Anderson Rea (Long Airdox)
The Greater Building Society
BHP Steel
Wellings Signs

CORPORATE SUPPORTERS

Ansett Australia
Apollo Charlestown
AT&T
Australia Post
Australian Geographic
Axcess Concrete Pumping
Barker Harle
Bilbie Whitford & Dan
Blackwoods
Blundell Trading
Boral Building
Boral Asphalt
Brambles Armoured

Brambles Industrial
Bulbeck's
Cambridge Press
Cleanaway
CMPS & F
Coopers and Lybrand
Copybind
Coursemaster Autopilots
Data Cabling Solutions
Doran Constructions
Dr Lieve Stassen
EJE Architecture
ELGAS

Everything Electrical
FH Compton & Sons
Framesi Australia
Gardner Perrot
Genetics Fitness Club
Gentlemen's Outfitters
GIO Australia
Greg Swane Constructions
Hillsborough Road Physiotherapy
Honeysuckle Development
Howard Smith Limited
Hunter Control
Hunter Village Health
IBM Newcastle
Jayes Travel
Kilpatrick Green
Lake Macquarie Yacht Club
Lindens Shoes
Macdiarmid Sails
Marathon Tyres
Maxwell Optical (Nikon)
Michillis Constructions
Mitre 10
MSB Hunter Ports
MSB Waterways
New World Honda
Newcastle Cardiac Services
Newcastle Cruising Yacht Club
Newcastle Day & Night Chemist

Newcastle 'Great Race' Committee
Newcastle Herald
Newcastle Speed Soccer
Newcastle Water Police
NRMA
Palmer Bruyn & Parker
Pasminco Metals Sulphide
Pioneer Concrete
Queens Wharf Brewery
Rite Lift Toyota
Robtec Engineering Products
Robtec—Allen Bradley
Rock City
Sanitarium Health Foods
Schaefer Marine
Sheather & Merrigan
Sony
Sparke Helmore
Steelmark Eagle & Globe
Steve Nebauer—A Bear Image
Suters Architects
Taxi Services Co-operative
The Anchorage Port Stephens
Thomas Laycock Solicitors
Trannys
Tubemakers Structural
Walkom Linehans
WHO Presentations

INDIVIDUAL SUPPORTERS

Andrew Lobb
Bill Corkhill
Bill Harder, Charleston
Bill Saddington
BOC Race Management Staff
Bruce Jones
Bruce Robertson
Bruce Robinson, Cape Town

Christian Life Centre, Macquarie
    Hills—friends
Craig and Alison Wellings
Dave and Diane Rankin, Tahiti
Dave Saddington
David Lyons
Don and Margie McIntyre
Frank and Jenny Davis, Canada

Fred and Ellen Baker, Charleston
Garth and Fiona Goodwin,
    Cape Town
George Snow
Glenn Currington
Glenn Willimmen, USA
Graeme Prosser
Graham Knock
Hernandez family, Charleston
Hilton and Beverley Grugeon
Ian Kiernan
Ian Macdiarmid
Jeanne Walls
Jeff and Donna Tousley, USA
Joe and Julie Epple, Charleston
John and Margaret McNaughton
John Church
John Griffiths
John Trevillian
Josh Hall, UK
Julie Christenson
Kanga and Beth Birtles
Kate Ford, USA
Laurel Goodwin, Cape Town
Louie DeBeer, Cape Town
Louise and David Bonsor
Martin Picard
Max and Janiece Smith
Merf Owen, UK

Mick Nebauer
Mike Hemmings, Cape Town
Mike Rabbitt
Nick King
Noel Jenkins
Paul Hannan
Peter and Hilary Heanly
Peter Barnes, Cape Town
Peter Pannys
Peter Routley
Phil and Robin Lee
Ralph and Ros Gourlay
Ray Dinnean
Richard Chapman
Rob Barker
Rob Barrett
Ron and Joy Robson
Ron and Shirley Nebauer
Rudder team, Uruguay
Scott Wallace, Charleston
Simonstown Yacht Club South
    Africa
Stephen Chapman
Steve and Maree Lamb
Steve and Marja Vance, USA
Susan Hiscock (late), UK
Tommy Michilis
True Blue team
Vanessa Smith

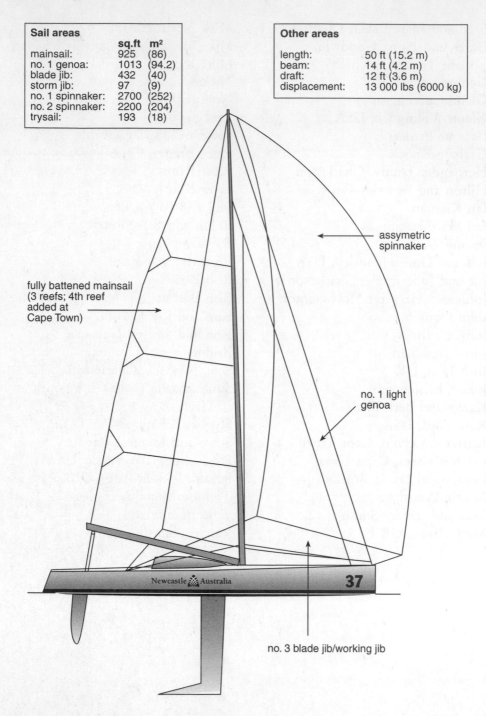

Sail areas

	sq.ft	m²
mainsail:	925	(86)
no. 1 genoa:	1013	(94.2)
blade jib:	432	(40)
storm jib:	97	(9)
no. 1 spinnaker:	2700	(252)
no. 2 spinnaker:	2200	(204)
trysail:	193	(18)

Other areas

length:	50 ft (15.2 m)
beam:	14 ft (4.2 m)
draft:	12 ft (3.6 m)
displacement:	13 000 lbs (6000 kg)

assymetric spinnaker

fully battened mainsail (3 reefs; 4th reef added at Cape Town)

no. 1 light genoa

Newcastle Australia

37

no. 3 blade jib/working jib

▲ *Sail plan of* Newcastle Australia

CHAPTER ONE

On my way

THERE was 30 minutes before the starting gun of the fourth BOC Challenge and it was time to say goodbye to my shore crew—my wife, Cindy, my younger brother, Mick, and my mentor and boatbuilder, Kanga Birtles, who had been on board *Newcastle Australia* for the tow out to the race starting area. It was a race rule that competitors had to be alone on their vessels 20 minutes before the official start of the 27 000 nautical mile race.

Having released the line from the 23 foot (7 m) towboat, I radioed race control to say that Cindy, Mick and Kanga were ready to be picked up in one of the official high-powered inflatable dinghies. This left me with only a few precious moments with them. The farewells were emotional. I hugged and kissed Cindy. We had shared some incredible experiences since we were married in 1987 and it was going to be hard to leave Cindy and our two children, five-year-old Annie and three-year-old Vance, for so long. But this was their race too and we had chosen this course for our life. So few people have been able to take part in this race that we felt we were indeed a privileged couple.

I hugged Mick and thanked him for his help. Mick had spent the past twelve months in Europe and had travelled to Charleston from Crete to help prepare the boat for the race. I felt like hugging Kanga but instead I grabbed his hand in a firm shake in an effort to communicate how much I appreciated his help and encouragement over the past few years. I wanted him to know how much his efforts had helped me to make it to Charleston. At the same time I was trying to absorb his last-minute pep talk. Kanga was as cool as ever—after all this was only a boat race—'I should get out there and give them heaps'.

▲ *Mick Nebauer, Kanga Birtles and myself on our way out to the start line*

I was now alone and milling about in the blustery south-westerly breeze with a reefed mainsail, getting a feel for the conditions and positioning *Newcastle Australia* for a reasonable place on the start line. I was as nervous as a cat.

Twenty competitors' vessels and several hundred spectator craft waited off the entrance to Charleston Harbor, South Carolina. The start line was marked at one end by a US Coast Guard cutter and at the other by a US Navy warship. Their size added to the drama of the pre-race maneuvers as the fleet jockeyed for position amid the many varied spectator vessels. It was 17 September 1994.

Now so close to the start, there was no time for emotion or nerves. I took hold of the wheel and my tension evaporated. This is what I had come for. I told myself not to worry about getting a textbook start but to go for clean air and room to maneuver. The last thing I wanted to happen, just for the sake of a few seconds, was a collision with another competitor or with an over-enthusiastic spectator boat—I had a long way to go.

Waiting for the 10-minute gun and trying not to crowd any of my rivals, I picked my spot and sailed out to the windward end of the line. Sailing back, I maintained boat speed to time my arrival at the line seconds after the gun sounded—the gun that was to send nineteen men and one woman heading around the world. Each was as serious as the others, each was there for different reasons—some to win, some just to get around, some with every chance of winning and some with slim chance of getting around. Where did I fit in? Where would I end up? I was determined simply to do my best.

The gun sounded and I felt a rush of adrenalin. The race had begun. I felt great excitement to be embarking on what had been a dream since I was a small boy—to sail solo around the world, a journey of over 27 000 miles. From the start I flashed past *Protect Our Sea Life*, a South African vessel and one of the smallest in the race. I then rapidly overtook Simone, a young Italian sailing the 50 foot (15.2 m) *Town of Cervia, Adriatic Sea*. This was wonderful. Then Jean Luc Van den Heede tore past me in his sleek red 60 foot (18.2 m) *Vendée Enterprises*. This was Jean Luc's fourth solo circumnavigation since 1986 and I wondered how he felt. I had long admired him and his exploits. It was great to be sailing alongside him.

▶

Newcastle Australia *off to a good start*
CHRISTOPHER AMER

At the starting line the water had been choppy because of wash from the spectator fleet but *Newcastle Australia* took off at about 10 knots, quickly leaving the wash-tub water behind. I was sailing on a marvellously flat sea with a moderate beam wind and *Newcastle Australia* flew. It seemed as if the boat had been waiting for this moment and was breathing a sigh of relief. For a time I was accompanied by a few hardy spectator boats with the people on board waving and yelling words of encouragement. My parents sped up to offer a final best-wishes wave. I could see Dad with a serious look in his eye, while Mum was grinning. They were holding Annie and Vance, who appeared ecstatic although not really sure what all the fuss was about. Nonetheless, they were delighted to be part of it. I could only wave back and try not to let this last glimpse of loved ones affect me—I had a job to do. This was the pinnacle of my sailing career.

The fleet spread out quickly as each skipper sailed the course that was felt to be more advantageous. I observed compatriot David Adams aboard the Class II favorite *True Blue* sailing lower with a spinnaker set, steadily passing the 60 foot (18.2 m) *Queen Anne's Battery*. I was content to sail a bit closer to the wind. With my big overlapping headsail and now full mainsail, *Newcastle Australia* was sailing at 11 knots and revelling in the conditions as land disappeared over the horizon. Astern were several of the other competitors and I was delighted to see two of the bigger Class I boats among them. I was off to a good start.

The BOC Challenge is made up of four legs. The first leg would take the fleet south-east across the North Atlantic Ocean to the equator where we would have to cross the doldrums, an area notorious for calms and fickle breezes. The doldrums, or intertropical convergence zone, divides the trade winds of the Northern and Southern Hemispheres. However, the frequent calms are occasionally interrupted with tropical squalls that threaten to overwhelm a vessel one minute only to leave it wallowing the next. This would be an area where tactics would become critically important. Competitors would try to get through with the minimum number of calms to give them the advantage to be the first to pick up the steady south-east trade winds of the South Atlantic Ocean. Then would come the days of constant pounding, bashing hard on the wind before being able to turn east and head for Cape Town and take advantage of the stronger westerly winds that would power the vessels on once they were south of the thirtieth parallel of latitude. With almost 8000 miles to sail to Cape Town, I hoped to reach the South African city in fewer than forty-two days.

The sky had shown ugly signs early on race day but once underway the weather cleared and it seemed that the further offshore I sailed the better it became. The wind had been forecast to drop soon after the start but it held beautifully at about 18 knots from the south-west and I pushed on, trimming sails and keeping the boat at its peak.

At 1630 hours on the first day, 4.5 hours after the starter's gun was fired, I was down below at the chart table, plotting my position, which I had read off my GPS (Global Positioning System) receiver. *Newcastle Australia* was sailing effortlessly averaging 10 knots. Suddenly, without any warning, there was a tremendous thump in the bows. I was thrown forward, hard against the table. The boat had hit something and lost all speed. I heard the unknown obstacle bump along the hull as the yacht regained momentum. Quickly I raced on deck. Looking aft, I could see a half-submerged raft, approximately 8 to 10 feet square (2.4 to 3 m square), rolling listlessly in my wake. I had sailed just more than 40 miles. To hit something so soon was devastating.

▲ *Cuban refugee raft similar to the one I hit. This photograph was taken off the coast of Florida en route to Charleston before the race start*

Immediately I inspected the boat for any damage and leaks. I started at the bow to check the point of impact. Working my way aft I realised, much to my relief, that there were no cracks or leaks. The boat was sailing well again but with a slightly reduced speed, and there was a steady 'bump, bump, bump' sound low in the hull. Peering over the side I was unable to see whether anything was caught on the keel or rudder. What could it be?

Had the platform ripped open the hull's outer fiberglass laminate? Was it flapping as *Newcastle Australia* sped along?

Obviously it needed a more serious inspection. It takes a lot to get me swimming so, hesitatingly, I lay on the side deck and, donning my diver's face mask, clung to the side rail and bent my body over the side of the boat until my head was in the water enough to see under the shallow hull of *Newcastle Australia*. I remember that the water was an incredible blue and as clear as crystal. To my relief I discovered that it was a length of rope with a piece of timber on either end that had broken away from the raft and become entangled around the rudder. Because of the buoyancy of the wood the rope was unable to drop off with the forward motion of the boat. It was the pieces of wood that had been banging against the hull. After dropping the sails and stalling the boat, and thus losing precious time, I was able to grab the flotsam and clear the debris. Due to the delay I had lost about an hour so, with a generous 18 to 20 knot breeze, I hauled up the sails and set off again. The full impact of this collision was not to become evident for another thirty days.

Meanwhile, Class I skipper Josh Hall, aboard *Gartmore Investment Managers*, had sailed up abeam of me, although about 2 miles to windward.

▲ *Part of the rope and timber from the raft that was wrapped around my rudder*

We sailed on at a similar speed as evening approached, marking the first of many nights at sea that the fleet would share over the next eight months.

Each vessel was fitted with a Comsat and Trimble Standard-C transmitter and antenna, which automatically transmitted information of the vessel's position via satellite to the race headquarters in Charleston as well as faxes and e-mail to home. Every morning all the skippers would receive an updated position report for the fleet based on this information. The skippers gained access to the reports through their laptop computers, which were connected to the Standard-C. The reports became a key ingredient when developing strategies and in the decision-making process for daily and overall tactics. The reports would often dictate the mood on board each yacht as they indicated gains or losses for each yacht's overall position for the previous 24 hours. There was delight at any advance and a gritting of teeth and a renewed effort to keep up a steady pace if ground had been lost.

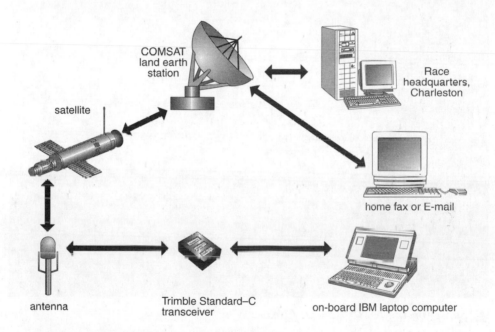

▲ *How my Comsat and Trimble Standard-C system worked*

By noon on the third day I had travelled 697 miles, averaging 230 miles a day noon to noon—good solid progress. For the first few days the wind had blown steadily from the south-west and enabled the fleet to make a great start. Isabelle Autissier, the only female competitor, was leading the group and was beginning to establish a strong lead by going far to the east.

I was in third place in Class II and had taken more of a southerly or rhumb line course, as had the majority of the sailors. However, the beautiful breeze that had sent us on our way with such perfect sailing conditions had been gradually fading through the third night as it backed towards the south and east.

At first the lighter conditions were fine and enjoyable: little did I know that the winds would continue to be light and variable until I was south of the equator. Still, the race was exciting, and the whole fleet was experiencing slow but pleasant conditions. Also, after a few days at sea the stress of the frantic activities ashore before the start began to ease and I began to enjoy the routine of being at sea. With the weather being ideal and being well-positioned in the fleet, life on board was wonderful.

▲ *Sunset on the North Atlantic Ocean*

Although the ideal scenario for me is to sail with Cindy because we live and work well together, to be responsible for the running of a yacht at sea on your own creates a different challenge. Being a Christian certainly gave me confidence and a healthy perspective on life, and I never go to sea with the view of being a conqueror or of taking on nature. The sea and the elements will always be bigger and tougher than people and ships. It was satisfying knowing that whatever happened to me during this voyage, and with my family at home, God would enable me to deal with it and to come through.

I was making steady, albeit slow, progress down across the North Atlantic Ocean and life on board had settled into an easy rhythm. After the exciting offshore blast of the first three days the boat began to idle along at about 120 to 170 miles a day. The slower progress was fine because everyone was experiencing similar conditions. I was in a group with David Adams on *True Blue*, who was leading to the east and south, Josh Hall on *Gartmore Investment Managers* to the south, and Niah Vaughan on *Jimroda II* to the north and west. I was to enjoy a fierce rivalry with Niah over the many months and miles to come.

Day followed day and soon we were counting our time out from Charleston in weeks. The positions in the fleet would change daily as a skipper, ahead of his rivals, would fall into a windless hole and others crept past in a breeze of their own. I would often hear skippers boasting in jest on the chat hour as to their extraordinary skills, only to find that the following day these same people were becalmed.

It was a game of skill mixed with chance. We would make decisions based on the weather information received and by observation of local conditions. Sometimes this would pay off with huge gains, and at other times with frustrating results. The north-east trade winds that were expected to blow in and allow us to sail fast toward our destination never materialized. Instead, the predominant winds stayed light from the east and south-east, the direction we wanted to go.

Isabelle Autissier on *Ecureuil Poitou Charentes 2*, JJ Provoyeur on *Ben Vio* (later called *Novell South Africa*) and Giovanni Soldini on *Kodak* had sailed a radically different course to the majority of the fleet and had great success sailing to the east while still further north. As a result they were leading the fleet. When the benefits of these tactics became apparent it caused a wave of indecision. Some of the boats further behind tried to recover some ground by leaving their original game plan and dashing to the east, only to wallow in calms for days. What had worked two weeks previously for the leaders would not necessarily work all of the time.

I was moving steadily closer to David Adams because I had managed to hold a light breeze while he struggled in calms to the south. I was thrilled to be in this race. It was fascinating, sailing as fast as conditions would allow, day and night. My daily runs would vary with the fickle wind—138, 156, 160 miles, occasionally even as poor as 67 miles—a far cry from the 190-mile average that I had hoped for on this leg. Every day was different as we ambled through the calm patches and then occasionally into a favorable area of stronger breeze. At these times *Newcastle Australia* would take off and we would fly at 8, 9 and sometimes 11-plus knots for hours at a time— just how it should be!

Intense concentration was needed to make the most of these conditions. I had difficulty establishing a regular rest and work pattern in the ever-changing light winds. Each variation of wind strength would mean constant sail adjustments. My large overlapping genoa would go up or down to be replaced with the smaller jib. And when the wind angle was favorable, up would go the big 3000 square feet (914.6 m square) white spinnaker with the name of our home port, Newcastle Australia, written boldly across it in red and green. Also, I could alter the trim of the boat by pumping water ballast to either side to suit. In effect this gave me the equivalent of 20 people sitting on the rail. I grabbed as many miles as possible.

Every day became an obsession with miles. I had to count down the distance to my next waypoint, which was the position I had selected to change direction for Cape Town, the distance to Cape Town, the distance I was ahead of *Gartmore Investment Managers* or *Jimroda II*, and the distance I was behind David or Christophe or Isabelle. I was constantly setting targets and goals and ticking them off as I went. My life was made up of components that fitted together and in the end, God willing, would result in a successful voyage. The first 1000 miles was ticked off, the first week at sea, the first 24-hour spinnaker run, the best distance run so far and so on. As goals were met new ones were set. These small achievements would be celebrated with a special treat for dinner, such as a prepackaged Chinese dish or an extra piece of fruit cake.

Meals, however, occupied only a brief part of my day. My culinary skills were far from lavish or creative and were all cooked on a two-burner propane stove. I mainly viewed food as a means to feed the human machine. Often dinner would be similar to yesterday's and finished in a matter of minutes. On this leg I found I ate a lot of rice and pasta dishes—tortellini became a favorite. I would cook enough to last two nights so that the next evening meal of leftovers would be quick and easy to prepare. Breakfast, which later became my main meal at about 1100 hours, usually consisted of eggs in various forms—cooked in a spicy Mexican salsa I always enjoy, or fried with my own version of hash browns. I used to dread it if one of the other skippers mentioned eating bacon for breakfast. I had no refrigeration on board and Cindy and I had been unable to find any bacon that would keep without refrigeration. I found it hard to go without one of my favorite foods for so long. For lunch and snacks I usually had tinned fruit, crackers, apples or oranges. In the middle of the night, fresh fruit was a delicious and healthy boost.

As the days blurred, I began to enjoy a simple solitary routine dictated by wind and weather conditions. My main concerns were boat speed, food and sleep. It was important to get enough rest and to maintain a balanced diet so as to remain fit. I knew that a lack of either or both could result in rapidly diminishing mental and physical stamina brought on by fatigue. It was important to pace myself and to ensure that I was able to sleep enough each day. I could not risk becoming exhausted, unable to deal with emergencies or troublesome conditions that could require me to be on deck for hours at a time.

I needed at least 5 to 6 hours of sleep a day as a minimum. This would often be broken up into catnaps of from 30 to 90 minutes during the night, depending on conditions. I found it important to get at least 30 minutes of sleep during the afternoons, which helped conserve my energy.

For each skipper the problems were similar. The routines and methods of sleeping and staying healthy, while attending to the demands of navigation and safe running of the boats, had to be dealt with in a personal manner and would be varied, just as each vessel was chosen and prepared in vastly different ways by each skipper. During David Adams's preparation he spent time with a sleep disorder specialist monitoring his sleep patterns to establish the best times for him to rest with maximum effect. The late Mike Plant, a veteran of the two previous BOC Challenges, used to sleep ashore with an alarm waking him every 20 minutes for several days prior to starting a race.

Even though conditions had been light, some of the boats were suffering setbacks. Neal Petersen, the young South African skipper of *Protect Our Sea Life*, had broken a forestay a few days into the race and he had to divert to Bermuda for repairs. On day 12, Mark Gatehouse, the skipper of *Queen Anne's Battery*, retired due to personal and business problems at home in England.

MIDNIGHT 29 SEPTEMBER
My log reads:

I have just received a fax from Mark Gatehouse wishing me well. He has withdrawn!!???

I had enjoyed meeting Mark and his wife, Patricia, in Charleston just before the start. I could not believe that he would retire. I was relating to all the work and effort that goes into a campaign. For me it was unthinkable not to finish what one had started, but each to their own. I hoped the decision was one Mark could live with as he was placed second in the fleet at the time. For some reason I found Mark's situation left me unsettled for several days.

It was reassuring to know *Newcastle Australia* was one of the most modern and well-equipped yachts afloat. However, our campaign was grossly underfunded from its inception. We had been able to find the money to launch the boat through fundraising and sponsorship, including a loan from Newcastle City Council, but there was no money for the actual race. Cindy and I had arrived in Charleston with US$15 after crossing the Pacific Ocean and the pressure from financial demands was to plague us the whole of the way around. It was vital that I be able to talk with Cindy.

Through my Standard-C, I was able to send Cindy, Annie and Vance a fax each day. This was a great way to stay in touch and find out how my family was going at home, and also to keep abreast of the business situation in Australia—the ongoing search for more sponsors and the financial input I desperately needed to keep racing.

Frustratingly for the first few weeks of leg one my communication with Cindy was one-sided. I could send faxes to her but she was unable to send a message to me as she had a problem with her computer and modem—essential ingredients in the link between us during each stage of the race. Each day I would be eagerly expecting the little green light on my terminal to light up, indicating mail had arrived. It was frustrating not knowing what was happening at home. I had tried a radio telephone link as I was desperate for news. With so much to discuss, I was dismayed by the US$300 cost. It was worth it but there was no money to do that regularly. I waited and I remember vividly the excitement at receiving my first message from Cindy and the relief of knowing that communication was again a two-way thing.

For each leg of the race radio schedules were conducted at 4-hourly intervals, which enabled the skippers to speak to each other via single sideband radios. These schedules were optional and affectionately known as the chat hour. I usually checked in each morning and again in the evening. The radio schedule was implemented as an opportunity to speak to someone other than yourself, if so desired. But more importantly it provided a safety network between competing vessels. If someone were in trouble, another competitor would be the closest means of rescue if that became necessary. In each of the previous three BOC Challenges this link had proven invaluable as rival skippers had been called upon to rescue a fellow competitor.

It was interesting to listen to other sailors discussing weather conditions and life on board. Often problems would be discussed, and the old saying would ring true that 'two heads are better than one' as suggestions or ideas were bandied about.

During these first weeks at sea a friendship was developing between Josh Hall and myself. Josh was sailing the Class I 60 foot (18.2 m) *Gartmore Investment Managers*. This was Josh's second BOC Challenge. He had competed in the 1990–91 race aboard *New Spirit of Ipswich* (now competing as *Jimroda II*), coming third in Class II. We found we had quite a few things in common, being similar in age, and our projects were similar in that we had a lot of smaller sponsors rather than one major sponsor. We even had a common sponsor. One of my major sponsors was the Newcastle office of Ernst & Young, and Josh was sponsored by this international company's Ipswich, England, office. Also we both had young children and our wives played a major role in running the campaigns in our absence. We were enjoying a close race with each other, our boats had similar speeds in some conditions and we found we were repeatedly crossing tracks. Several times, unaware of Josh's position, I'd go on deck to discover his sails on the horizon or masthead navigation light in the distance during the night. I'd be delighted to see him astern of me, but at other times he might have the advantage, which would lead to renewed vigor on my part to check the trim or crowd on sail in an effort to put him back in his place.

▲ *Niah Vaughan on* Jimroda II, *with whom I enjoyed a healthy rivalry*
STEVE NEBAUER, A BEAR IMAGE

It was great to be sailing against a Class I yacht but the real job was to keep my eye on the other Class II boats, mainly David Adams on *True Blue*, who was ahead of me by between 30 and 50 miles for much of the first few weeks, and Niah on *Jimroda II*, who was persistently a threat to my third place. Niah was poised to swallow me if I had problems or made a mistake.

I remember BOC's elder statesman, Harry Mitchell, commenting on how much he enjoyed listening to Josh and I speaking on the radio. Apparently he found our conversations about our families and the struggles with our campaigns entertaining. Harry was 70 years of age and one of the characters of the group, sailing the 40 foot (12.2 m) *Henry Hornblower* in his third BOC attempt. I think we all admired his dogged determination to be a part of this race.

As interesting as it was to keep in touch with some of the skippers, I found the radio schedules frustrating and distracting. All of this modern equipment was new to me. In my previous fifteen years at sea I had never had a radio. I felt that to not come up during the chat hour regularly could mean that I would be seen as aloof and snobbish, so in my efforts to be friendly I would naïvely reveal information about my position and the weather that could then be used to advantage by some of my rivals.

And I was enjoying some fantastic sailing, the sort you normally only read about—days with sunny skies and moonlit nights, warm enough not to need anything more than a T-shirt at night. Due to the light winds my daily average was way down from what was expected or needed for a fast first leg and already the fleet was probably five or more days behind target. By day 22 I had sailed 3520 nautical miles at an average speed of 6.6 knots, or 160 miles a day. This was not brilliant but was good considering the percentage of light unfavorable winds we had experienced. *Newcastle Australia* was proving herself to be a beautiful boat, well-behaved and easily driven. The racing was always exciting and challenging. I never grew tired of the constantly changing scene of ocean and sky that contained my world.

0100 3 OCTOBER
My log reads:

Already sailed 115 nm since noon, which is fantastic (considering the recent slow progress). I can't remember such consistent breeze, steady 17.8 knots it's great! Earlier tonight I was so exhilarated by being here and God's goodness I could hardly sleep.

However, by now I was getting closer to the doldrums and beginning to experience fluky winds and more unstable cloud patterns. Tropical thunderclouds became more frequent and the winds unpredictable as squalls moved through. It was amazing how much of an effect these localized weather systems had on my progress. For example, one morning when Josh and I were in sight of each other, I went to the east of a cloud and Josh to the west. By mid afternoon we were 30 miles apart, each experiencing different conditions either side of the cloud. That particular day it went in favor of me and gave me the edge. The next time it could easily be the other way round.

So far my voyage had been easy. Nothing had gone wrong with the equipment on board and my main frustration had been the lighter than expected winds and communication problems. This was about to change. On the morning of 4 October I had a nap from 0830 until 0900 hours and, upon rising and going on deck, I was devastated to discover that the masthead forestay with the light number one genoa (furled at the time) had disconnected from the bow fitting, and the 75 foot (22.8 m) length of wire and rolled sail was whipping dangerously off to leeward. It was connected to the boat only by the furling control line and the masthead fitting. The turnbuckle had broken at the end of the threaded stud used to tension the forestay. I thanked God that the wind had eased off as I raced forward to secure the gear to the bow rail. I could ill-afford to be long without my big lightweight headsail. I would need to find a more permanent solution. Fortunately, I had a spare stay in the aft compartment and was able to find an extra turnbuckle stud that was stored with it. Remembering the old cliché that it could have been worse, much worse, I was soon able to reconnect the fitting and it was business as usual. I certainly kept a wary eye on fittings after that incident.

Later that same day my propane stove began to run erratically. The flame was weak and spluttering. The main tank normally lasted eight weeks or so. I was sure my brother Mick had refilled it before the start. I changed tanks and it ran for a few minutes and then showed problems again. I knew that the tank had enough propane. It became a priority to determine the problem. Further testing showed there was no gas getting through to the burner, and this indicated that there was a problem with the regulator that controlled the pressure of the propane through the system. I tried bypassing the regulator with almost catastrophic results. Flames shot out like an acetylene cutting torch. I quickly shut it off. With no replacement I dreaded the prospect of cold food for the remainder of the leg.

On the evening radio schedule I asked Niah and Josh if they had ever had a similar experience, only to be the butt of some British humor. They were actually concerned but the problem was mine. I woke the next morning determined to find a solution. I had nothing to lose so I began to strip the regulator. Laying out my tools and the parts with the ritual of a surgeon about to begin a delicate procedure, I opened the aluminium housing of the regulator to find the valve mechanism inside had corroded badly. This was causing a blockage. I was able to scrape the corrosion out with my knife and sprayed the components with a light oil. After reassembling the unit I hooked it up and was ecstatic when it worked perfectly once again. I made a note to order a replacement regulator, which Cindy could bring to Cape Town. Both of these problems were pretty simple but could easily have been the cause of much misery.

By now my immediate goal was to get to the equator and into the Southern Hemisphere. I was starting to feel trapped by the North Atlantic Ocean and its fickle breezes, although I could hardly complain—life was very pleasant and if only I would be patient and keep concentrating *Newcastle Australia* would soon have me in the South Atlantic Ocean rushing toward Cape Town through the hopefully more reliable south-east trades.

9 OCTOBER
My log reads:

Well you wouldn't believe it!!! Position report has me 7 miles closer to Cape Town than David Adams (I bet he is ticked off). I looked and thought it had me 7 behind until Niah called me up and said 'congratulations you're second'. I didn't believe him.

My moment of glory was short-lived, however, as the wind was such that the best course I could lay was to the east. I held that tack longer than I should have and sailed right into a hole of zero wind. It was unbelievable. I was ahead of Niah and even Josh at the time and could do nothing but watch as their position reports indicated that they were holding their breeze and sailing by. I felt incredible pressure from that mistake and worked and worked for three days to extract myself from that blunder. I had little sleep as I continuously had to chase and make use of every zephyr that came my way. I was encouraged when the windless hole I was in extended and caught up with Niah and Josh. I certainly never wished a foul wind on my competitors but I still had a chance if they had similar conditions. *Newcastle*

Australia is light, only weighing six tons, which meant she would have better speed in the drifting conditions than my English adversaries' older and heavier boats.

Those three days seemed to last an eternity. Finally I began to get a breeze that allowed me to begin sailing again. It actually began as a gentle north-easterly that gradually backed through the west to the south-south-west. It was a headwind but wind nonetheless. It felt good to be moving. I had been able to pull Niah and Josh back as they struggled in a similar windless patch. Sailing fast again the world was a much nicer place! The equator was 270 miles away—come on down!

The wind kept swinging until it settled into the south-south-east around 18 knots. I was making rapid progress on a port tack. Back in third place of Class II it was good to be alive! The weather still appeared unstable and I sailed on under an overcast, angry sky.

1800 13 OCTOBER
My log reads:

Across the equator ... at 1656 local time. Praise the Lord!!! Have been banging away since yesterday morning in this confounded headsea, headwind ... 26 days to reach equator? Should have taken 20 max! Anyway am into Southern Hemisphere finally!!

Cape Town was a touch over 3500 miles away.

CHAPTER TWO

Rescue at sea

Across the equator at last! What a relief. It was a real boost to be in the Southern Hemisphere again. I felt like I was back on my own turf. The reality was, however, that I still had several weeks of sailing ahead of me before I could expect to reach Cape Town. It was amazing that, as I crossed the line dividing the Northern and Southern Hemispheres, the weather and sky took on a whole new attitude. I looked back and could clearly see a line separating the black clouds that had been my companions for the past week or so from the clearing blue sky south of where the imaginary line called the equator would be.

The south-east trade winds quickly established a steady rhythm—literally a breath of fresh air. The course to steer was south and the lines of latitude began to roll rapidly by. It was exciting to have finally left the trying North Atlantic Ocean with its fickle calms and headwinds. Although I complain about the North Atlantic Ocean it would have to be the most pleasant ocean to sail.

The breeze at between 18 and 25 knots of true wind continued to provide a fast ride. I was sailing almost hard on the breeze, easily sitting on between 9.4 and 10.4 knots. In these conditions *Newcastle Australia* began to show her true colors and flew south, steadily pulling ahead of Niah on *Jimroda II*. How quickly I forgot the slow going of the previous month. As the other boats began to get the fresher trade winds with the rougher sailing it was not long before I began to hear complaints on the radio schedules about the lack of comfort due to the yachts heeling more. The conditions made it harder to do routine chores on board, and perhaps in Nigel's case aboard *Skycatcher*, there was the added risk of spilling champagne as he set down his glass to change a compact disc.

18

Not long after crossing the equator, Josh on *Gartmore Investment Managers* had slipped past me and was making a good show of it in the more reliable breeze, with his boat's heavier displacement and longer waterline length suiting the fresher conditions. The two boats settled into a groove and pounded on south at similar speeds, different classes of boats but with both skippers trying to outdo the other. My plan was to stay close enough to Josh so that if conditions changed suitably I could slip past. *Newcastle Australia*'s light weight would then be an advantage. We enjoyed the competition and rivalry, continuing to chat at least once a day.

▲ Gartmore Investment Managers *before the start of the race*

During these first few days in the south-east trades the moon was full, providing excellent night visibility. My favorite spot at night was to stand at the stern of *Newcastle Australia* and lean on the running backstays. Looking ahead from the cockpit, *Newcastle Australia* made a splendid sight as she sailed as fast as possible, gracefully threading her way south, taking the endless swells in her stride, with only the occasional pound or moan from the highly tuned hull and rig. I marvelled that a boat made from components of foam, glass and resin could be such a powerful machine—almost a living thing.

These romantic interludes, however, were often interrupted with rude awakenings as sheets of flying spray would shoot aft and soak me, but in these tropical southern latitudes it was not much of a problem getting a soaking. Later, in the higher latitudes of the Southern Ocean, bursts of freezing spray would not be so much fun. They would need to be avoided, not just for the sake of comfort but to reduce the risk of losing energy through exposure while working on deck in the extreme conditions.

Newcastle Australia was beating south, chasing degrees, twenty-nine days into leg one. My plan was to continue south until reaching my waypoint at 30 degrees south 20 degrees west, at which point I could expect the help of westerly winds and could begin to alter course for Cape Town. However, this waypoint was still over 1000 miles away and I could look forward to at least five to seven days of ceaseless pounding before I could turn the corner and head east to Table Bay.

It was an exciting time. *Newcastle Australia* was working beautifully. It was bumpy but I was enjoying the leg immensely. All my equipment was working well except for a problem that developed with an alternator on my diesel generator that I ran to produce electricity. However, I was able to replace this with the spare alternator and this would see me through to Cape Town.

Some of the other skippers were not so fortunate: old Minoru on *Shuten-Dohji II* had severe leaks and was diverting to the small port of Cabedelo in Brazil for repairs; Christophe on *Sceta Calberson* had lost all communications and his autopilots when his generator seized and had to hand-steer much of the last half of this leg, sometimes as much as 20 hours a day.

During this period south of the equator my log mentions my concern at an apparent reduced boat speed. I was still going well but felt that the boat did not have the same speed and was unable to put my finger on the problem. The reason was to become obvious very soon.

On the evening of 17 October at about 1800 local time I was preparing my dinner (canned stew) and bashing away on a port tack at about 9 knots. I was stirring the pot when I realised that I was a bit late for the evening radio schedule. I remember thinking that I would give it a miss because I did not really feel the need to speak to anyone. I was content to enjoy the solitude of the twilight, my favorite time of the day, and perhaps would tune in on the next schedule. However, curiosity got the better of me and as I tuned the set in the darkened cabin, illuminated only by the glow from the back-lit instruments on my desk, I came in halfway through a sentence by Nigel on *Skycatcher*:

🎙 *'Alan to contact HQ immediately, I don't know why. Pete sent me a message on the Standard-C. Has anyone heard from him?'*

This certainly peaked my curiosity.

🎙 *'Skycatcher this is Newcastle. Over.'*

'Oh, Newcastle ... this is Skycatcher. Can you call Pete at HQ urgently. I don't know what is up, only that you are to contact them immediately. I think they are standing by on 16. Over.'

'Thanks Nigel, I'll try 16 now. Over.'

I tuned in on the higher long-distance frequency that would send my voice to the communication trailer in Charleston, almost 5000 miles over the horizon. Maybe Cindy had sent me a message via Pete Dunning at race headquarters?

🎙 *'K X E 221 BOC control this is Victor Hotel November 5086, do you copy? VHN 5086 Newcastle Australia.'*

'KXE 221 to Newcastle. Divert to Josh! Alan divert to Josh! He is sinking. Over.'

What incredible news! It seemed unreal that Josh was on his boat and in trouble. I was able to get Josh's latest position from headquarters and said I would head for him and contact Josh by radio so that we could co-ordinate our rendezvous. The office could monitor our relative positions via the satellite terminals that each boat was fitted with. I was 84 miles from Josh on a course of 155 degrees true—hard on the wind. I radioed race headquarters with an ETA of around 9 hours time, about 0300 hours, knowing that they could only sit tight and observe what was happening through their computer terminals. I was praying and I think there were a few new believers in the communications trailer and among the fleet that night. I also sent Cindy a fax:

▶ -- ◀

Cindy, Josh is sinking. I'm nearest, 84 miles. Please pray. Love Al.

▶ -- ◀

I felt numb at the news that Josh had hit something and that *Gartmore Investment Managers* was going down. It was hard to relate to such a drama occurring on what had seemed to be a friendly sea. I contacted Josh on the radio but our initial conversation was tense and to the point. Josh gave his position and briefly described how he had dropped off a wave while hand-steering and had landed on something that had punctured *Gartmore Investment Managers'* hull about a third of the way back from the bow, flooding the two forward compartments. The damage was such that Josh was unable to stem the flow of water, even after trying to pack the damaged area with spare sails shored up with floorboards and whatever else was available. A sailor's worst nightmare had begun.

Josh and I exchanged positions and agreed to speak on the radio every half hour so that I could monitor his position for the rendezvous and keep abreast of the on-board situation. I would need to keep a recent record of his position in case his batteries failed or he had to abandon ship and get into his life raft before I arrived.

Josh sounded stressed but certainly not in a panic. His bilge pumps were pumping furiously. *Gartmore Investment Managers* was equipped with some very large bilge pumps, including an engine-driven one that could pump 660 gallons (2500 L) every 7 to 8 minutes. Josh and I later calculated that, with several electric pumps and the big engine-driven pump operating flat out, at their specified capacities he was pumping more than 4000 gallons (15 000 L) of water every hour.

I put *Newcastle Australia* onto her new course with the sheets hardened on for the work to windward. Fortunately, I would not have to tack to reach Josh. Josh had dropped sails to stop *Gartmore Investment Managers* and was struggling to gybe the foundering vessel downwind to allow her to drift towards the north-west. This would mean I would have to sail a lesser distance so that I was able to sail off the breeze slightly to gain some more speed.

Josh and I spoke briefly a couple of times on our half-hourly schedule. You could almost feel the tension of the other skippers as they huddled in front of their own radios listening for details of Josh's predicament as the drama unfolded.

With 9 hours to reach Josh the rescue became a waiting game. *Newcastle Australia* was going as fast as the conditions would allow. There was not much more I could do except concentrate on my navigation and ensure that the boat speed was maintained. I reheated and finished my interrupted evening meal and tried to get a few minutes sleep between schedules with Josh. It was going to be a long night.

I had left the radio on and occasionally I could hear some of the other skippers speaking to each other in hushed tones as if it would appear irreverent to speak normally. Thirty minutes would go by quickly and it would be time to check in with Josh again. Normally it would take only a few seconds before he would respond to my call and broadcast his latest position. However, at our schedule time at 2200 hours when I called Josh he did not answer.

'Gartmore this is Newcastle . . . Gartmore this is Newcastle.'

Several minutes with no reply and the tension was mounting.

'Gartmore this is Newcastle. Are you there Josh? Come in mate!'

There was no response. Images of *Gartmore Investment Managers* disappearing and Josh in his life raft, or worse, flashed through my mind. Repeated calls brought no answer.

I became very concerned after at least half an hour of repeated calls to Josh with no reply. I asked Nigel of *Skycatcher*, who was standing by to relay messages if necessary, to try calling Josh. Again repeated calls brought no response. By this stage we were all feeling pretty grim and all that I could do was to keep going as fast as I could toward what I had calculated would be Josh's position—and I still had 5 hours of sailing ahead of me.

It was to be another hour before Josh could get back to his radio and the fleet was allowed a big sigh of relief. He had been working in the forward part of *Gartmore Investment Managers* pumping and trying to control the gushing water, losing track of time before finally hearing my repeated calls above the noise of his engine-driven bilge pumps.

'Sorry mate, I was pumping.'

We exchanged positions and Josh promised to be on the air promptly in another 30 minutes.

Meanwhile, I was having problems of my own. *Newcastle Australia* had appeared sluggish earlier in the night but I had put it down to my anxiety and the urgency of the situation. Now the boat was definitely off the pace. Instead of 9 to 10 knots of boat speed, I was having trouble staying above 8 knots. I thought I was trying too hard, expecting too much from the yacht. The trim was fine and the breeze was steady at about 21 knots. Maybe I had some weed or a net on the keel?

With the bright moonlight breaking through the clouds I peered over the side and I was able to see into the water down to the black painted keel. To my horror I could see that the fiberglass fairing around the keel had broken away and was creating a huge drag. I could not believe it! I was in the middle of a crisis, needing all the speed and maneuvrability that the boat could muster and the keel fairing was disintegrating.

◀

Newcastle Australia *about to be launched at Newcastle in June 1994. Her keel is a rectangular steel structural beam projecting 12 feet (3.7 m) from the hull with a lead ballast bulb*

Newcastle Australia's keel was a rectangular steel structural beam that projected 12 feet (3.7 m) from the hull with a lead ballast bulb connected to it. Its sleek foil shape was made up of symmetrical molded fiberglass halves joined at the leading and trailing edges of the keel. Perhaps, I thought, the damage resulted from my collision with the Cuban raft on day one of the race. The accumulated flexing over the intervening 5000 miles and the pounding through seas in the south-east trades had caused the keel to split down the back of the molded fiberglass fairing, which allowed the two halves to open out as wing flaps on an aircraft. Apart from causing a severe loss of speed, the turbulence made it difficult to steer the boat. It posed no threat structurally but was to have a huge effect on *Newcastle Australia*'s performance for the remainder of the leg.

Now aware of why I was losing boat speed, my most pressing concern became to get to Josh's sinking boat as soon as possible. Josh and I continued to check in every half hour. I would plot his position on my chart so that I could closely monitor our relative positions and make any adjustments to my course if needed. Josh sounded pretty good considering his predicament— it must have been an incredibly nerve-racking time for him.

The modern communication systems on board the yachts made the crisis seem almost unreal. Josh, up to his waist in water, would be interrupted by a telephone ringing. Josh's Satcom-M satellite-link telephone provided him with a direct-dial worldwide telephone link via satellite so that at random intervals during this crisis his telephone would ring. Often it was a British or US Coast Guard checking to see how he was. One of the calls was from Josh's brother at home in England. Alan, upon hearing of his brother's plight, felt the need to speak to him but was speechless due to the seriousness of the situation and only managed to ask 'How's your sinking going?'.

With Josh's drift in my direction and with *Newcastle Australia*'s boat speed of about 8 knots, the gap between the vessels was closing at a speed of about 11 knots. My original ETA of between 0200 and 0300 hours was looking good.

I suddenly remembered that it had been exactly thirty days since I had last seen another human being and that, as there was not much I could do, perhaps I should employ the time by tidying up the boat and making myself presentable. I was nervous at the prospect of having someone else on board. Despite the fact that I usually washed every day and in warm weather had a saltwater bath on deck, I decided I should shave and have a sponge bath so as not to risk offending Josh by giving him the impression that Aussies were unkempt when left on their own for a while.

As Josh and I drew nearer we began to check in more frequently so we would not run past each other in the night. I was monitoring my radar screen for a sighting of *Gartmore Investment Managers* and at about midnight a large target suddenly appeared on the radar screen. Eager about our approaching rendezvous but knowing that it was too soon to be Josh I called him on the radio and said that I thought I had him on radar. As I spoke the target on my screen moved towards me at an alarming rate and increased in size. I tore out on deck to discover that the radar had detected a small squall cloud several miles distant. Feeling rather foolish by the false alarm I continued on my course.

Finally, at 0130 on 18 October, at a distance of 12 miles, *Gartmore Investment Managers* appeared as a strong target on my radar screen. About 10 minutes later her masthead navigation lights came into view. I was quietly ecstatic and sent up a few thankyou prayers because I had arrived in time to help.

I called a relieved Josh and we decided that he should send up a distress flare so that I could positively identify him. It would have been a waste of precious time to have eased my course toward the vessel if it had not been Josh. Soon Josh had my lights in sight. We began to speak on our handheld VHF radios as the closing stage would need me on deck for maneuvring. After the hours of tension throughout the darkness, and now with the vessels finally in sight, it seemed as if we were racing toward one another at a terrific pace. I furled my headsail and put a slab reef in my mainsail to reduce the sail area and to slow *Newcastle Australia* down. With reduced sail I would have less to deal with and she would be easier to handle during the pick up. However, as I reefed the mainsail I suddenly saw that *Gartmore Investment Managers* was abeam of me by about two boat lengths off my starboard side. Josh probably thought I was a tourist as I sailed on by. I hurriedly finished reefing and left a mess of ropes in the cockpit to be sorted out later. Then I gybed and headed back to Josh.

By now Josh had given up the futile pumping and was on deck preparing to board the life raft that he had inflated and lashed alongside for the transfer. My first sight of *Gartmore Investment Managers* as she drifted, low in the water hampered by the weight of the flooded compartments, sent a chill up my spine. It was eerie. The stricken vessel, illuminated by moonlight and the glow of the navigation lights, became a sight I would not forget.

With the 10 foot (3 m) seas that were running it was impossible to come alongside *Gartmore Investment Managers*. Josh and I had earlier agreed that the safest way for him to board *Newcastle Australia* would be for him to drift away from his yacht in his life raft and for me to pick him up from the life raft. Easier said than done. Not long after I was on station and had made a dummy run past Josh to get a feel for the conditions, he abandoned his yacht. He climbed into his orange and black rubber raft leaving behind the dreams and efforts of the past four years and drifted into *Gartmore Investment Managers*' wake. However, the life raft remained attached to the yacht by a length of line and when the raft reached the end of its tether the momentum from the yacht's drift threatened to overturn it. I sailed up to Josh and threw a line to him. However, feeling that the raft was about to flip, Josh ignored my line, grabbed a knife and cut the umbilical cord to *Gartmore Investment Managers*.

Alone and suddenly adrift in the middle of the night in such a flimsy craft Josh must have felt incredibly vulnerable. I sailed by and had to tack and gybe *Newcastle Australia* back into position. To make matters worse, all this twisting and turning was causing the damaged keel fairing to open further, increasing the drag and making *Newcastle Australia* very sluggish to answer her helm. Momentarily losing sight of the raft among the swell, my heart was in my mouth as I sailed back for another attempt.

Finally after another attempt I successfully passed a line to Josh. Letting go of the wheel, I raced aft to haul him aboard through my open trench-style cockpit. The floor of this was conveniently the same height as the edge of Josh's raft, which made it easier to grab his hand and heave him on deck with a hearty 'welcome aboard'. Josh smiled, relieved and thankful.

As he slumped against the side of the cockpit neither of us really knew what to say—we were both a little stunned. I set about retrieving some of the gear that he had salvaged and brought across in the life raft. I had to kneel on my cockpit floor and reach down into the bottom of the raft. Grabbing one of the bags I fell head first into the life raft from which Josh had so enthusiastically exited only seconds before. My legs were on deck and my head and torso were in the raft. With *Newcastle Australia* drifting along at a few knots I felt in quite a predicament. Josh snapped to attention and, grabbing my jacket, hauled me aboard. We both had a laugh which eased the sombre mood.

My first priority now became to get Josh a warm meal because he had not eaten during his ordeal. How quickly circumstances can change. Fewer than 12 hours before Josh had been blasting along at 10 knots enjoying a solitary adventure with hardly a care in the world. His yacht, the result of ambition and 4 years of determined effort, was crippled and about to disappear forever in depths of about 5000 feet (1525 m). Neither of us wanted to witness *Gartmore Investment Managers'* final moments. So, after chatting quietly on deck for a while and releasing the life raft that we had slashed so it would sink, I hoisted the mainsail and reset the jib, again heading *Newcastle Australia* on course for Cape Town. We continued to watch *Gartmore Investment Managers'* masthead light until it was out of sight.

CHAPTER THREE

The dynamic duo

ONCE Josh was on board, we notified a jubilant Pete Dunning at race headquarters that the rescue was a success. Josh telephoned home and let his wife Laura and family know that he was safely berthed on *Newcastle Australia*. Everyone was ecstatic. I called Cindy, it being late afternoon in Australia. The timing was such that we even did an interview with one of my sponsors, NBN Television—they got the scoop and the story went to air on their evening news, broadcast within a couple of hours of Josh's pick up.

After a month of being on my own it was strange to suddenly have another person on board. This being a single-handed yacht race meant that Josh could not take part in the running of the boat. To be suddenly out of the race and on another boat, having to resign himself to being a passenger as well as dealing with the personal loss involved, was quite an adjustment to make.

Since Josh's pick up my keel had been causing even more drag as the broken fairing had splayed out more. Now the boat would only sail at about 5 knots. The last thing Josh needed to hear was that my keel was falling apart. I did not tell him about the keel problem until after the rescue. However, once on board it was obvious to him that something was wrong. As we stowed Josh's salvaged gear we found water sloshing around in the shallow floor of *Newcastle Australia*, there being no floorboards or bilge, and it was blatantly obvious that we had a leak. Josh was relieved for the activity when I handed him a bucket and a sponge asking him if he would bail the boat out!

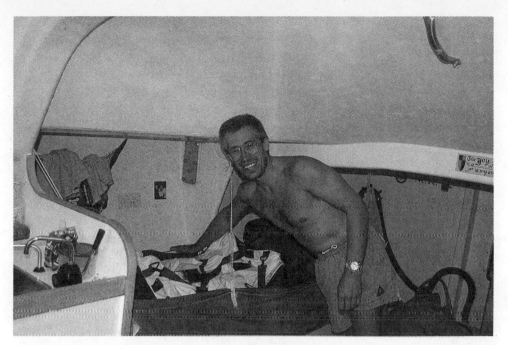

▲ *Josh stowing his gear away once on board* Newcastle Australia

The leak turned out to be from the internal metal support that housed the keel inside the boat. When the fiberglass fairing was twisting and breaking loose it allowed water up the keel box which leaked into the cabin. After identifying the problem, I was able to smear the outside of the box with a bedding compound that provided a temporary solution to such an irritating problem.

With the leak taken care of for now, the next thing on the agenda was what to do about the keel? My original thin foil-shaped keel was now a giant V-shape, creating huge drag. With so much turbulence it took about a quarter of a turn on the steering wheel to make the boat head in a straight line. It was still dark and both Josh and I needed a break so I decided to wait until later in the morning to tackle the problem and plodded on like a cripple for a couple of hours. I decided to see if I could break the shattered fairing off and free *Newcastle Australia* of the hideous appendage. The best way to do this was to tack the boat constantly. I even backwinded the sails and reversed the yacht until suddenly there was a thump as the broken pieces finally released their grip, plunging to the bottom of the Atlantic Ocean.

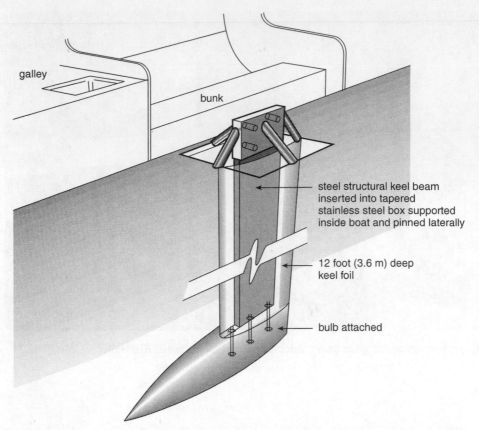

galley

bunk

steel structural keel beam
inserted into tapered
stainless steel box supported
inside boat and pinned laterally

12 foot (3.6 m) deep
keel foil

bulb attached

▲ *How the keel was attached to the hull of* Newcastle Australia. *When the foil tore off, the original seal at the site of hull penetration was destroyed and water leaked from the top of the keel box*

Released from her burden *Newcastle Australia* seemed to surge ahead. However, now we were sailing with a keel that was only a rectangular steel beam about four inches (10 cm) thick that provided stability but no lift, having lost all hydrodynamic properties. It was to become apparent that *Newcastle Australia* now faced about a 30 per cent reduction in performance.

The morning after Josh's rescue I calculated that we had thirteen to fifteen days sailing left until Cape Town. Little did Josh and I realise that we would be at sea together for just on three weeks in a yacht that was sparsely fitted out. *Newcastle Australia* had only two bunks and Josh made his home in the main cabin on the port side settee, while I was relegated aft to the under-deck quarter berth.

I felt terrible for Josh. He was physically fine having suffered no injuries but it would take some time to adjust to the trauma and the finality that

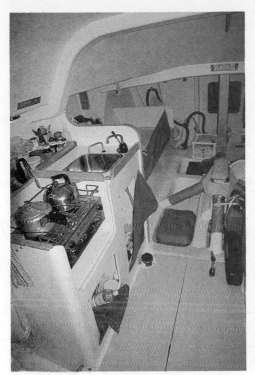

▲ *This shot of the interior of the yacht shows the shallow floor of Newcastle Australia. The water was leaking in through the keel box*

▲ *Once the foil had torn off, my keel was purely a steel structural beam with a lead ballast bulb. This resulted in a 30 per cent reduction in performance*

his race was over. I credit Josh for not falling into despair—he handled everything really well, maintaining a good attitude. His wife Laura was at home in England with their son Sam and pregnant with their second child and Josh took solace from knowing that in a few weeks he would be reunited with them. He began to look ahead in earnest to their reunion in Cape Town.

To resist boredom and fulfil media/sponsor commitments, Josh became the world's best communicator, spending quite a bit of time each day on the radio or the Standard-C. He took over the radio schedules—being the man of the hour everyone wanted to chat with him. There was an endless list of media requesting interviews and first-hand accounts of the sinking of *Gartmore Investment Managers*.

We received quite a few faxes and notes of encouragement and congratulations. One was from Tony Lush who, as a competitor in the first BOC Challenge in 1982, was rescued in the Southern Ocean after his yacht was rolled and sunk. As self-proclaimed Grand Poo-Bah he awarded Josh lifetime membership of the 'Single-handed Sinkers Society'.

When I was called to assist Josh my arch rival Niah had been 120 miles behind. Now he began steadily to eat away at my lead. Sailing in conditions in which *Newcastle Australia* should normally average 210 to 230 miles a day, Josh and I were faced with depressing results. Each day at noon I calculated the distance sailed for the previous 24 hours. It was discouraging to see that we were losing at least 40 to 50 miles per day to the other sailors who were further behind. Toward the end of the leg the winds dropped for several days and the percentage effect of the drag from the keel was to escalate, causing even greater loss of speed—and consequently even greater frustration.

About four days after the rescue 'Old Niah' on *Jimroda II* snuck past the handicapped *Newcastle Australia*. You could see Niah smiling over the radio—he did not miss an opportunity to gloat about his victory over the 'dynamic duo', as Josh and I had become known. It was all I could do not to pull my hair out from the frustration of falling back into fourth place in Class II. I still had seven Class II boats and one Class I boat behind me but it became hard to remain motivated and keep racing the sluggish and unresponsive *Newcastle Australia*. From a competitive viewpoint this leg became written off and my goal now became to get to Cape Town with enough time to make repairs and start afresh for leg two.

As there was always the search for more funds, with the boat needing a haul out and keel repairs in Cape Town, the pressure was increased. I would contact Cindy on the radio every night for an update and she would tell me of her struggles to find income to keep the campaign going, let alone money for repairs. It looked as though she would not have the money to fly to South Africa for the stopover. Some people in Australia were even putting pressure on Cindy to wind up the campaign, citing that the odds were against me and that *Newcastle Australia* would be the next boat to sink! It seemed hopeless.

However, by the grace of God we had made it this far. Cindy and I were always confident that I would finish the BOC Challenge. We just were not sure how or when this major hurdle of lack of money would be overcome. We could only take it one day at a time.

In true form, things worked out at the last minute. *Sports Illustrated* in the United States offered to buy an article from Josh and I on the rescue.

My share took care of most of Cindy's and the children's airfares. An Australian yachtsman who had previously made an offer to help if needed responded instantly and generously to a fax to his office suggesting that now would be as good a time as any.

All of the radio telephone calls to home and media were expensive, at about US$8 per minute. However, another blessing came to me during this time in the form of a sponsorship deal with the American communications company AT&T. Josh had been testing an AT&T direct-dial modem connected to his single sideband radio. The modem allowed him direct-dial telephone contact for the race. It was slightly restricted in comparison to satellite, which enabled direct-dial anywhere at any time irrespective of atmospheric conditions, but by matching the frequency to the propagation conditions you could make clear direct calls worldwide. Now that Josh was out of the race, AT&T offered to fit *Newcastle Australia* with a direct-dial modem and handset on arrival in Cape Town and free air time. In the meantime we could both make unlimited calls home using the standard manual link method through the AT&T operators in New Jersey. For the rest of the race this was a great benefit in keeping up to date with my family and business at home. As part of the testing program I would check in with Glenn Willimmen at AT&T for propagation and signal tests weekly.

Josh and I got on remarkably well for two eccentric solo sailors. It took me several days to settle down and get used to another person being on the boat. My normal sleeping pattern was totally disrupted. Usually I would nap for half an hour in the morning and again in the afternoon but with Josh on board and after a month of solitude we could not stop talking to each other. However, I missed my routine and being able to pace myself and became extremely tired. Our throats were red raw from overloading our, until now, little-used vocal chords. It took about five days before I could put my head down during the day for a nap and begin to re-establish more of a normal working and rest pattern.

The following days became tedious. Josh was out of the race and should not have been here. I was disappointed with my placing. We needed a gale to get decent speeds and as the winds dropped off our spirits tended to drop off with them. You could have described us as unhappy campers.

However, during these days of frustration and adjustment there were times of excitement. As we finally reached 30 degrees south and began to run east in stronger favorable breezes our mood elevated. On one occasion *Newcastle Australia* forced her damaged keel through the water to achieve a day's run of 220 miles, which was outstanding given the handicap.

After a week or so of Josh being on board we had established a routine. We shared the cooking, with Josh preparing most of the lunches. But by now after thirty-eight days at sea most of the interesting food was gone. There were only a few oranges and some apples left when Josh arrived, so we would stretch these out by cutting them and each having a half. Josh developed a speciality dish of pasta with a cheese sauce mixed with tuna—it looked terrible. I wondered if they ate like this in England. The concoction tasted almost reasonable if you ate it quickly. After eating it for several consecutive days, however, I began to lose my appetite mid morning. I had been out of sweets for some time and had requested Josh to save some from his yacht. He had brought with him a box of forty Mars bars and each day we enjoyed one with our afternoon cup of tea.

On 24 October Isabelle Autissier from France made history by becoming the first lady to win a leg of the BOC Challenge. She sailed her 60 foot (18.2 m) *Ecureuil Poitou Charentes 2* into Table Bay after an incredible voyage of only thirty-five days eight hours, smashing all previous records for the leg by about two and a half days. By sailing a radical course and establishing an early lead that she never relinquished, Isabelle made some brilliant moves that put her into Cape Town five days ahead of the nearest competitor, Steve Pettingill on *Hunters Child*, still with almost 1000 miles to go.

On board *Newcastle Australia* we were excited for Isabelle and the others as they began to arrive in Cape Town but it really drove home the fact that we still had 2000 miles to go in a crippled boat. We took one day at a time as we plodded on but by now the winds had become fluky and often from the east. What had happened to the westerlies? On we sailed, taking things as they came and always hoping that the conditions would improve.

David Adams arrived in Cape Town to win Class II for a 'true blue' Australian victory in just over forty-two days. David had sailed brilliantly, beating several Class I boats. He was followed 23 hours later by Giovanni on *Kodak*.

Once all the front-runners were in Cape Town, the weather window traditionally closed for us still at sea. As *Newcastle Australia* sailed into a hole of light winds it seemed that this leg was meant to be a lesson in endurance. The meals were becoming very boring and my log holds fascinating comments about our culinary delights—'noodles again!!!'. Several days followed where my daily runs were way down. On one occasion we only covered 62.4 miles in 24 hours. It was maddening. I felt really sorry for Josh and would often apologise for his forced detention. He was great and often it was he who would encourage me.

While it probably helped to have someone on board to vent my frustration with, I had no respite from the work of running a small ship at sea. Day after day I had to continue to sail solo, which meant taking care of maintenance and navigation, as well as dealing with often interrupted sleep. Waking for sail drill in the middle of the night (why is it always a crisis at 0200?), on one occasion I found myself on deck struggling to deal with a wild spinnaker that was overdue in being taken down. Precariously balanced on the foredeck trying to tame the huge nylon sail, I became chuffed, thinking that good manners should dictate and that it would be nice to have a hand at this particular moment. My passenger blissfully slept on.

With huge relief we broke the 1000 mile barrier to Cape Town, which now seemed almost within reach. It was almost time for our families to leave for their flights to South Africa. Knowing that our wives would soon be heading toward us was a real boost and Josh and I began to feel that the end was in sight.

Via the Standard-C I began to arrange hauling the boat out of the water for keel repairs. We needed details from the yacht's designer in Sydney and Cindy could pick them up before her flight and bring them with her to Cape Town. Our good friends, Garth and Fiona Goodwin, who lived 300 miles (500 km) from Cape Town, were planning to take time off from their forestry business to help with the job list. Josh offered to help out too once he had spent some time with his family. I started to get excited about fixing the boat and looked forward to the prospect of doing well in leg two.

'Old Niah' continued to maintain a lead over me and, of course, never let up reminding me of his skill and cunning abilities. Niah and Nigel had made a wager that the loser between the two of them would buy the other a meal at the Mount Nelson, one of Cape Town's oldest and most prestigious restaurants. When Josh and I heard them on the radio discussing entrees and vintage wines we promptly invited ourselves and our wives to make up a party. I am not sure how we got away with it but graciously we were all to enjoy a fantastic night out at that classic establishment at Nigel's expense.

However, on day 48 an ecstatic Niah Vaughan arrived off the breakwater at Cape Town and instantly disappeared from the radio banter. The silence was deafening. Josh and I still had over 400 miles to go. We were sliding around in zephyrs of wind on a greasy, smooth, flat sea the color of slate. Would we ever arrive?

That night the breeze began to fill as another cold front moved in from the west. We began to sail again and so we started to discuss the prospect of arriving in Cape Town. This breeze lasted for only a couple of days to then be replaced by another windless hole and we wallowed with only 160 miles to go. Patience was at a premium as we lay 'becalmed again'.

Newcastle Australia was placed between Arnie Taylor on the Class I *Thursday's Child*, who was to the south of me sailing in 15 knot southerly winds, and Nigel to the west, who was reporting 20 knots from the north. Josh and I were incredulous as we sat in zero wind praying for a break.

The break finally came as another front approached bringing with it a near gale from the north-north-west. As dawn broke on 8 November, my fifty-second day at sea, we had 92 miles to go. The sea was a dirty grey color and the sky a matching overcast. But we were moving. *Newcastle Australia* was still below her normal speed but she seemed to have a bone in her teeth as she romped along, over and through the harsh chop that had developed once we were sailing in the shallower waters of the continental shelf.

With about 4 hours left to sail I, magnanimously, decided to make Josh a celebratory cup of coffee. While lighting up the propane stove to boil the water, I was dismayed to see a splutter of blue flame as I ignited the burner. On trying to light it again I realised that we had finally run out of propane. We both had a laugh as with land almost in sight it was no great drama to go without hot food or drinks, but it was cutting it fine.

Josh was ecstatic as we approached and he spent hours on deck peering ahead through the grey mist. Several hours later he was rewarded with the first sight of land when, at 1530 hours local time and at a distance of about 10 miles, the profiles of the Lions Head and Green Point became visible through the clearing grey mist. I had expected my first sight of Cape Town would be with the backdrop of classic Table Mountain but, with the low grey overcast, to see these lesser landmarks appear was just as much of a thrill.

We were now within VHF radio range and we were speaking to BOC control at the Royal Cape Yacht Club. Cindy, Laura and our children were on board a 40 foot (12.2 m) motor launch that was making its way out to us through the chop. What a thrill it was to finally be here! My position in the fleet was a bit dull, but we had a long way to go still and I could now only enjoy the fact that we were here and I was competing in this exciting event. God willing I would do better in the next leg.

As we neared the breakwater and the buoy that marked the finish line we could see our wives and children waving through the spray-covered windows of the launch. What a moment that was! Cindy and Annie and Vance were beaming across the water at me—I think I was oblivious to anything else for a while. The decks of the boat were crowded with media

▲ *Herb McCormick, Josh Hall and Mark Schrader aboard* Newcastle Australia *immediately after crossing the finishing line in Cape Town*

photographers and journalists, along with a contingent of officials and enthusiasts. Niah Vaughan was on the aft deck, jacketed from the spray, with an ear-to-ear grin on his rogue's face, giving me the thumbs up. Next time, I thought!

It then sank in that this first stage of my great adventure was about to close. I received a message that an inflatable dinghy would pick Josh up so that I could sail across the line solo. I took affront at this and in defense replied that Josh had just sailed the leg and was entitled to finish it too. So, at approximately 1730 local time, the dynamic duo took the gun for fourth place in Class II.

Immediately after crossing the finish line, *Newcastle Australia* was boarded by the BOC race director, Mark Schrader, and BOC media man, Herb McCormick. It was great to see these two. Also jumping on board were some crew from the huge red inflatable dinghy that moments before had enthusiastically slammed up alongside me to assist with connecting the tow line. I was nervous at these strangers suddenly appearing and assuming authority over my vessel and I dashed forward to supervise, not giving them the credit due. After a few moments the sails were down and *Newcastle Australia* was safely under tow.

It was bliss to be able to wave over to Cindy—she is an amazing person and I felt like a kid in a candy store. I could not even concentrate on the hamburger she had thoughtfully sent over but sat it on the deck only for it to be trashed by someone's foot rushing past. We were towed into the Victoria Alfred Docks to a reception of about two to three hundred people lining the sea wall, some holding banners of greeting, all of them smiling huge smiles. It was amazing and totally unexpected to be welcomed so enthusiastically. Neither Josh nor I could believe it.

Once docked my responsibilities for the boat could relax a little, at least for a while. We were overwhelmed by the reception and I literally had to barge my way over to the launch that transported Cindy and the children. My son was sound asleep. I was embarrassed by the onlookers but it was wonderful to hug and kiss Cindy and Annie after so long. We had arrived.

CHAPTER FOUR

Cape Town stopover

I WAS allowed only a brief reunion with Cindy and the children before Josh and I were rushed into a room to give a first-hand account of the rescue and the ensuing weeks spent together. The media lapped up the fact that we had run out of propane and were down to 3.4 gallons (13 L) of drinking water and only basic food items such as rice and pasta.

This was a very emotional time for Josh. Apart from the relief of seeing his family again, the reality of being out of the race really hit home. Up until then, even though a passenger on *Newcastle Australia*, Josh was still intimately involved with the race. He was talking on the radio schedules and enjoying the camaraderie, the tension and excitement of the race, as well as the highs and lows of ocean voyaging. Suddenly, all this had come to an end for the second time in three weeks—it must have been extremely hard for him.

The leg two restart was scheduled for the afternoon of 26 November. This meant I had eighteen days in which to prepare the boat and spend a little time with my family.

Cape Town was a great place to be. I had looked forward to visiting the Cape area for many years and to be there was very satisfying. Because of my delayed arrival my time there would pass rapidly with so much to do to prepare the boat for my forthcoming Southern Ocean sojourn.

Our stay was made particularly enjoyable by the hospitality that we received there. Some people from nearby Somerset West lent us a car, and our friends Garth and Fiona Goodwin lent us a small cottage in the suburb of Wynburg. It was a treat to have our own place to go home to and to enjoy some quiet family time.

My main task while in Cape Town was to repair the keel. I arranged for the boat to be pulled out of the water and I was able to come to an arrangement with JJ Provoyeur, skipper of the Class I entry *Novell South Africa*, who was also the owner of Action Yachting, a marine repair facility located at the Royal Cape Yacht Club. JJ deferred payment of most of my repairs until the fleet arrived in Sydney. This was most convenient and allowed us more time to raise the money for the remainder of the stopover costs.

I found the transition from being at sea, combined with the sudden demands of a young family and being responsible for co-ordinating the repairs on the boat quite frustrating. My first few days were spent running around

▲ *Annie, a willing helper*

trying to source materials and technicians to help with some of the more specialized equipment on the boat. I was distracted and torn between the need to relax with my family and my commitment to the 'job list'. Consequently, for the first part of our stay I was not very productive in either department. It would have been more effective to have forgotten the race for a while and to have spent some quality time with Cindy and the children before tackling the tasks with renewed enthusiasm and a clearer mind. Regardless, we did manage to enjoy our time together amid the work schedule and the children still talk about the 'wildebeest' and other animals they saw there.

We hauled the boat out on the Yacht Club railway and work began on the keel. With the yard contracted to repair the keel, we took the opportunity to head up the coast for the weekend. We drove to Knysna, about 300 miles (500 km) east of Cape Town, where Garth and Fiona have a pine plantation. It was delightful to spend a couple of days in their small cabin with a view over the surrounding forest and hills. Garth and I drove back, leaving the women with the children for an extra day or two. We had met Garth and Fiona years before in Canada while Cindy and I were cruising there in our yacht *Deus Regit II*. It was fantastic to catch up with them and to accept their offer of help and accommodation.

▲ *The repair work on the keel was done at the yard of the Royal Cape Yacht Club*

Back in Cape Town work on the keel progressed in African time, slowly but surely. Garth and I set about tending the smaller items on the list. There were sails to be repaired and the generator needed a service with a new alternator installed, and one of the batteries had to be replaced. The rig needed tuning but that had to wait until the boat was back in the water. Josh called in and spent some time making up a net bin in the forepeak to stow the spinnakers better.

▲ *Garth Goodwin helping out with the job list*

Nigel had kept his part of the wager with Niah and booked a table for six at the famous Mount Nelson. I felt the part of an imposter, having not been in on the bet properly, but when the time came to leave for the restaurant Cindy and I were as keen as any to go. We agreed to meet at the Yacht Club and drive up together in one car. For some reason it was suggested that we go in our loan car. Unbeknown to Nigel, who normally drives a black turbo Porsche, the car we had borrowed was a faded red 1970 model Mazda. I can still see the stunned look in his eye once he realized he was to be chauffeured to the grand old Mount Nellie 'in . . . in that thing!'.

Mustering all the courage he could, he scrunched himself into the cracked vinyl back seat of the twenty-four-year-old car. We all clambered in after him and drove off in a festive mood. On arrival at the classic hotel we drove up a colonnaded avenue and parked in the covered foyer area. As our group extracted themselves from the two-door vehicle, one of the uniformed attendants marched up and not so politely told us we could not park there. Nigel, having recovered his composure and, dressed in an expensive Italian suit and looking every bit the gentleman, redeemed the situation. In his clipped British accent he politely requested valet parking for our vehicle and the surprised attendant took our keys and stepped aside to allow us entry to the grand old building. The Mount Nellie was everything we expected and we all had a wonderful evening.

Five days before the restart *Newcastle Australia* finally went back into the water. We had been making good progress with most of the jobs. The remaining items should have been straightforward enough but when the technician came to install AT&T's telephone modem there was some confusion regarding interference to the single sideband radio. The hours of testing then became days of re-routing cables. I was unable to get my own jobs done because the cabin was so crowded so by the time the technician had finished I was left with two days to sort out the mess, stow provisions and finish off the loose ends. What had been a reasonable workload became a nightmare race to meet the restart deadline.

Another pressure developed when the riggers came to tune and adjust the mast and rigging, only to discover a kink in the mast about 25 feet (7.6 m) off the deck. Their verdict was that the mast needed sleeving, that is, it needed additional support by bolting or riveting extra aluminium to the mast to increase the wall thickness and strength. To do this they would have to pull the mast out of the boat and reinstall it in time for the restart. With less than 72 hours before the restart we had no time or money for this option. I was unable to locate the company that had made the mast so, after consulting the designer back in Australia, we decided to proceed on the basis that the mast was larger in section than it theoretically needed to be and had not given any trouble during the previous leg. I was a little unnerved but trusted that it would be alright for the Southern Ocean leg to Sydney.

Meanwhile Cindy and Fiona were busy buying provisions for my next leg and stowing them away. The following is a list of the items they bought.

- 25 prepackaged ultra heat treated long life meals, such as Chinese dishes, roast beef, chicken with gravy and curry beef

- 7 dozen eggs
- 4 loaves of fresh bread and several packets of par-baked bread rolls to be heated up in the pressure cooker
- assorted crackers and biscuits
- assorted soups, mostly dry but some canned
- 20 packs of 2-minute noodles
- 4.4 lb (2 kg) of rice
- several 0.5 lb (250 g) packs of pasta, such as tortellini
- 5 cans of corn and a few cans of tuna
- Sanitarium Weet-bix supplied in individual portions of two to a pack
- assorted Sanitarium nuts and dried fruit, such as sultanas and apricots
- 18 pints (10 L) of long life milk in 1 pint (500 mL) cartons
- Neo Life—an energy drink added to milk that is a meal in itself and an excellent vitamin supplement
- cans of V8 vegetable juice—very high in vitamins
- 40 0.5 pint (250 mL) fruit juices
- 20 cans of soft drink
- tea, coffee and hot chocolate
- 40 oranges, 50 apples, 12 onions and 20 potatoes
- canned fruit
- candy and chocolate
- Power bars—high-energy food to help keep you going without a break
- 30 gallons (140 L) of drinking water

One of the highlights of the stopover turned out to be the awards night function on the eve of the restart. In the middle of all the last minute fuss I was obliged to down tools and drive several miles to attend the prize-giving ceremony. Unfortunately, I was not in the mood for a cocktail party and, arriving late and slipping into some jeans in the car park, we went in just before the formalities began. However, it turned out to be quite a special event.

Isabelle Autissier, the first woman ever to win a leg of the BOC Challenge, was presented with her first place prize to tumultuous applause. Each competitor received a momento for completing the leg. In turn, I was called to the stage to receive my inscribed plaque. However, as I left the stage I was told to go to one side and wait for instructions. Bewildered, I was called forward again. To my amazement I was presented with the leg one award for 'outstanding seamanship' in recognition of my rescue of Josh Hall. As I left the stage I was called again, this time to receive the 'Comsat communications award' for correct use of satellite and radio equipment

▲ *Fiona Goodwin and Cindy labelling and stowing my provisions in Cape Town*

▲ *Isabelle Autissier demonstrating the survival suit that she wore during her ordeal while waiting to be rescued*

during the leg, most notably during the lead up to the rescue of Josh. It was an honor to be recognized in front of the hundreds of people in attendance and among the other competitors, all of whose achievements I admire.

Once the prize-giving was over it was back to the boat for some more sorting out. Unfortunately, all the electrical work on the boat had disturbed my autopilots. I was still battling to reprogram them and not having much luck. Oh, how I longed to be ready 24 hours before the start so that I could relax quietly with Cindy, Annie and Vance. At midnight I went on strike and drove home to the cottage in Wynburg.

All too soon, however, I was back on board *Newcastle Australia*. My priority was to fix the autopilots. Thankfully, this major frustration turned out to be a minor adjustment, which was not specifically mentioned in the edition of the manual that I had on board. In minutes after telephoning Paul and Richard at Coursemaster Autopilots in Australia the problem was gone.

Wow, I actually had a few hours up my sleeve before the race start. Garth was a great help and sorted out the sails and the running rigging while I was able to spend some time with Cindy and the children before I was due to be towed out to the starting area.

▲ *On my way out to* Newcastle Australia *for the start of leg two with Cindy* BILLY BLACK

CHAPTER FIVE

Heading home

At 1500 hours on Saturday, 26 November to the sound of a cannon blast leg two began in earnest. The route was from Cape Town to Sydney 'by any seaward course leaving a waypoint at 53 degrees south, 119 degrees east to starboard'. The waypoint, which was on a parallel to the south of Heard Island, was set to keep the fleet out of the higher density areas of ice further south. Once past the waypoint, we had the option to head south and take advantage of sailing closer to the shorter and faster 'great circle' track to Sydney.

The wind was blowing at 15 to 20 knots from the south-west and the fleet of seventeen yachts had to work to windward out of Table Bay. Once clear of the Bay I went onto the southerly tack that would allow me to clear the Cape of Good Hope. I did not expect to see land again until closing the coast of Australia in Bass Strait, 6000 miles away. The wind eased for a while at sunset but picked up in strength later in the night so the fleet were making rapid progress. *Newcastle Australia* was close-reaching with the wind slightly forward of the beam, making between 10 and 11 knots.

The speed difference from the last leg was amazing. The keel repairs had worked well and to have good boat speed and control were a luxury. However, during the evening I ran the generator, only to discover that one of my alternators was not producing charge. I had two alternators permanently mounted on the small diesel generator and they had both been fine before the restart, one of them being new. If the second alternator held up my generator would be able to produce electricity for the leg but I was not happy at not having a back-up when heading into the Southern Ocean.

By 0400 hours the next morning I had sailed 130 miles from Cape Town. I started the generator and was furiously disappointed to realise that now my second alternator was not producing charge. After checking the connections, hoping that it might be something simple like a loose wire, I realized that there was no need for a decision. I had no choice but to head back. I radioed Niah Vaughan who was not too far behind me and told him of my predicament, also asking him for the telephone number of his mate Bruce, an electrical technician from Cape Town. Niah wished me well as he moved into third place. I went on deck and tacked *Newcastle Australia* about, laying the course for the Cape of Good Hope.

Waiting for a more reasonable hour (0630 hours), I then telephoned Garth, who suggested that I make for Simonstown, 60 miles to the north of me, a small naval town located in the lee of the Cape of Good Hope on False Bay. He would contact Bruce and meet me there. I telephoned Cindy and told her the disappointing news. She was not due to fly out that day and said she would meet me in Simonstown for lunch.

The trip back was fast although I did not experience any of the thrill normally associated with a landfall when I found myself off the breakwater at 1130 hours. A launch belonging to the local rescue authority kindly came out and gave me a tow in, although I did not appreciate the chap on board who threw me a line weighted by a heavy steel shackle. Dodging missiles, I was finally able to attach their line to *Newcastle Australia* for the tow to a berth at the yacht club.

Garth was there minutes after my arrival, followed by Bruce who was accompanied by Peter Barnes, the mechanic from Enza Marine. Enza Marine had worked on the generator during the stopover and Peter had come out to help if he could. Cindy was also there with the children. It seemed like ages since I had left Cape Town and I was very tired from not having slept while racing on the coast all night. After describing the problem to Bruce and Peter I went with my family to grab a bite to eat and find a place for an hour's sleep. I was exhausted and really feeling the pressure of the fleet blasting off with favorable conditions.

At 1730 hours Bruce and Peter gave the all clear. They had discovered a problem that had overloaded the switches used to change from one alternator to the other. This had created a blockage in the system, resulting in zero charge. I hastily cast off, thanking the guys for their help. For the second time in as many days I farewelled my family, determined to get back to sea and to try and recover my losses.

By the time I was sailing again the race had been in progress for 27 hours. My rivals had been sailing at an average speed of, say, 10 knots for that period, covering about 270 nautical miles on their course. My delay translated into a loss of at least 200 miles on the fleet at that early stage. It was maddening to think about.

On leaving Simonstown the wind swung more to the south, which meant a 20 mile beat to windward to clear Cape Point, the last land between me and the Antarctic continent. I had been exhausted ashore while waiting for the verdict on the repairs but once sailing again I felt strangely revived, probably with relief to be underway.

Once clear of land I had expected to be sailing fast on the heels of the fleet but instead I found myself in a different weather pattern. Before my forced stop I was enjoying a fresh south-west wind but now it blew southerly tending to the south-south-east at 23 knots true. This further increased my losses as my best course was over 50 degrees off the direct path that the other boats had been able to hold. We had far to go and I tried to keep a good attitude but I am sure that I sounded pretty bleak once I started to check in on the chat hour again. By the end of the fourth day I was more than 400 miles behind *Kodak* and *True Blue* who were enjoying a tight match race at the top of Class II. *Jimroda II* was 300 miles ahead and I made it my immediate goal to get out of last position and back into third place as soon as possible.

The sailing was rough and uncomfortable but it was not until the sixth day that I got my first true taste of a roaring forties gale. For the previous 24 hours I had been in light south to easterly winds and fog but early in the morning the wind shifted and began to build from the north and west. It was not long before the wind was up to 20 knots and then 30 knots, and *Newcastle Australia* began to sail before the building gale at terrific speeds. After the slow first leg it was exhilarating to be surfing before the wind and seas at steady speeds in the high teens—15 to 18 knots with bursts up to 24 knots displayed on the digital speedometer. Soon the wind was up to and over 45 knots. The pace was electrifying and *Newcastle Australia* was handling it well. It continued to blow all that day and the next.

That first blow did me the world of good. To that point I had been feeling intimidated by the thought of the Southern Ocean and the weeks that lay ahead. But with that gale the cobwebs cleared and I became more enthused and began to push the boat harder.

On 2 December the fleet was appalled to hear the news that Isabelle Autissier had been dismasted. I imagined what it must be like for her to deal with that deep in the Southern Ocean on her own. David Adams was not far behind and he diverted to see if she was alright. Apparently it was blowing a gale with reduced visibility in the sleet and rain. Isabelle did not want any assistance and waved David on his way. She planned a small jury-rigged mast and intended to make her way 1200 miles to the French-owned Kerguelen Island. I am sure it was with a heavy heart that David turned *True Blue* downwind and resumed racing.

Four days later the fleet was again jarred by news that Neal on *Protect Our Sea Life* had also been dismasted. He was limping back to Port Elizabeth in South Africa. Earlier the same week Arnie Taylor on *Thursday's Child* had lost his rudder but he was continuing on, sailing well with an emergency rudder. The attrition rate was much higher than anyone would have thought reasonable—as if the roaring forties were not intimidating enough without these dramas unfolding.

Once again a bizarre contrast was evident. Trouble had struck Isabelle, one of the most highly funded campaigns, along with Neal, who was sailing one of the least suitable entries.

Aboard *Newcastle Australia* my gear was holding up well. With all of the carnage in the fleet I was probably sailing more conservatively than I would have wanted. I was confident of regaining third place and realistically understood that I would not be able to beat David or Giovanni short of them having catastrophic gear failure. Their lead had increased even further, while I sailed for several days in untypically light, variable winds.

▲ *Southern Ocean scene while the weather was calm*

My route was to take me 6000 miles across some of the world's roughest seas. I was heading south and east across the Indian Ocean. My plan was to pass north of the Prince Edward Islands and below the Crozet Islands. On reaching 50 degrees south I would head basically in an easterly direction between Kerguelen and Heard Islands at a latitude of about 51 degrees south until reaching 120 degrees west. From there I could change course toward Bass Strait and the remaining 560 miles to Sydney.

Looking forward to reaching Sydney was an exciting prospect. Not only was it a couple of hours from my home in Newcastle but also on reaching Sydney I would cross my outbound track that would conclude my first circumnavigation of the world. I had left Sydney only six months earlier to sail to Charleston for the race, crossing the Pacific Ocean via New Zealand and Tahiti and then transiting the Panama Canal before arriving in Charleston in early September. Legs one and two would complete my circuit of the globe.

I was making some steady daily runs, averaging about 220 miles a day sailing in fog with a north wind at 23 knots. Gradually I began to pull back the boats ahead of me. A little everyday was all I could hope for and I would have to work patiently toward getting my third place back. If I could maintain consistent speeds and sail further south, thereby covering a shorter distance, it should start to pay off.

As I sailed deeper south the wind took on an icy feel and good thermal clothing became paramount, as was keeping dry when working on deck. I had some rubber dishwashing gloves on board and I found them to be the best solution for keeping my hands dry. I would wear them inside a pair of leather sailing gloves for protection, with the flexible rubber for waterproofing. It was an excellent and simple combination. As long as my hands stayed dry the cold was bearable. The few times I was caught outside without them my hands would burn from the cold. When I started working outside I wore a layer of thermal clothing next to my skin, with a polar tec jacket and ski pants on under my waterproof outer garments.

By day 14 I had sailed 2700 miles toward Sydney and had worked my way back up through the fleet to fourth spot in Class II—third place was within my grasp. Niah on *Jimroda II* was 20 miles ahead, sailing about 4 degrees north of me. I had been averaging 11.25 knots for over 30 hours in wind from the west-north-west at a solid 40 knots. With three reefs in the mainsail and a tiny headsail set we tore along hour after hour through sleet and drizzle. The furious fifties were living up to their name. *Newcastle Australia* was balancing beautifully. For a few days now the seas had been running at over 20 feet (6 m) but amazingly had kept an even distance between crests, allowing fast and quite safe progress.

With a front moving through the wind began to change direction, causing the swells to become confused and uncomfortable. As the seas became more confused they would heap up on each other, increasing in size and ferocity. More frequently cross-seas would crash into the boat sending her violently down into the troughs, the violent motion making it difficult to maintain the steady progress.

The afternoon found me standing fully clothed near the companionway. I had a clear view of the instrument panel at the navigation station and outside at the seas. I was preparing to go on deck when there was a sudden roar and crack! *Newcastle Australia* was slammed sideways embroiled in the seething crest of another breaking sea. The boat quickly recovered from the pummel, carrying on as if nothing had happened. During the roll the end of the boom gouged a trench in the sea taking the high-speed force of tons of water on the leech of the mainsail. Looking out of the cabin window I could see that the mainsail had a 6 to 8 foot (1.8 to 2.4 m) vertical tear at the third reef point, rending the sail useless until I could effect a major repair.

Dousing the mainsail in such conditions was difficult, with the gale pressing the folds of dacron against the mast and rigging. I was forced to continue on under a jib only at a more subdued 8 to 9 knots. The irony of it all was that within 4 hours the fury of the gale was spent and the wind steadily decreased during the night.

By morning I was in a 20-knot westerly sailing with the two headsails out wing-and-wing to catch the breeze. I was determined to get some mainsail back up as soon as possible. The dawn was grey but without the spray and heavy mist it was fairly dry on deck. Grateful that the conditions had eased, I began to flake the damaged sail on deck. I was not too keen at the prospect of a day outside in the almost freezing conditions, but with the effort to balance securely on the cabin top and stretching to do the repair I soon began to warm up.

To fix the mainsail became the most important thing in my small, self-contained world. I was blessed with a dry day and by mid morning the sun was actually shining for the first time in ten days and the afternoon was quite pleasant. *Newcastle Australia* was poking along at between 7 and 8 knots and every hour at this reduced speed meant that *Jimroda II* would be taking miles from me. After more than 9 hours and countless pricked fingers the job was as complete as it could be and I headed the boat into the wind to raise the sail. My jagged repair left the sail puckered and wrinkled. All the same, it looked beautiful as I bore away with the sail filling with wind and the boat came alive again, my speed increasing with the added sail area.

Unfortunately, the repair was fragile. I could use it in a moderate breeze but when the wind puffed up beyond 25 knots I had to reduce the area to the fourth reef, which was above the damage, so that it would not blow out all together. I had to nurse the sail and for the remainder of the leg in conditions below gale force I was under-canvassed.

I was more than a little perturbed the following day when I also noticed that the seam on the foot of my big genoa had split—it was not my week for sails. But now we were back in fresh winds and sleet so it would have to wait for a calm day before I could even attempt to lower it from the roller furling forestay.

Jimroda II had now gained more than 60 miles on me in the time it had taken me to repair the mainsail. It was to take me another two days before I could draw even and finally overtake Niah to claim back third place. However, I now felt like I was beginning to get somewhere. I set a new waypoint and course to the entrance of Bass Strait, 2709 miles away. With 560 miles to cover from Bass Strait to Sydney—a total distance to finish of 3269 miles—I was nearly halfway home.

Rummaging in my galley locker one evening I stumbled onto a box containing individual portions of a hot chocolate drink mix that came complete with a little foil pouch containing tiny freeze-dried marshmallows. It turned out that it was leftovers from my friend Garth's 1993 successful Cape to Rio race campaign. I only had to add water and pop in the mini-marshmallows and they would seemingly inflate and float on top, the combination making a delicious warm treat. I calculated that the box contained enough servings to allow me to introduce a nightly ritual and for the remainder of this southern leg I would have a cup as I listened to the evening radio schedule. Simple, but it certainly added value to the cold bleak life I was enjoying (?) at the time.

In fact, we were running fast in snow and westerly gales with consistent winds of between 30 and 40 knots. About one week after discovering the ripped genoa I managed, during a lull, to retrieve the sail from its furler and spent another day at sewing. This time though I was able to take the sail below into the relative comfort of the cabin and partially dry it out over my rarely used propane heater. I again had to wait several days for the wind to drop off so that I could repeat the process and reinstall the sail hoisted back onto the furling gear.

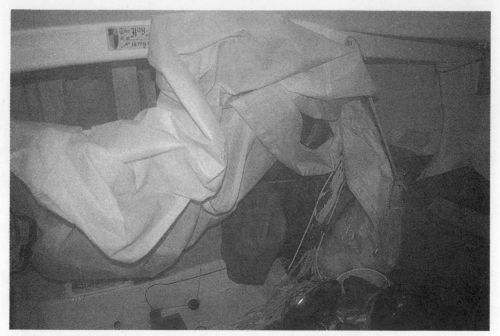

▲ *Drying out the genoa down below using my propane heater*

In port this is an easy task but at sea by myself, running before the wind, I would have to flake the genoa on deck and quickly haul the sail up the thin alloy extrusion. Every now and then the sail would threaten to blow over the side and this would cause it to jam in the luff groove. I would then have to race from my place at the mast, where I was hauling on the halyard, to tame the sail before it fell over into the water as this would have caused a real problem. Eventually, after some frantic foredeck activity, the sail was safely in place and ready for use. The mainsail repair was still intact and it was a relief to have all my sails once again available, even if they were getting tired.

These sail problems were frustrating my daily average. More often than not I would have to sail with less sail than was desirable. I could not risk any more damage to the mainsail and as a result I spent a lot of time with four reefs in when three would have been perfect. The gap was too wide between the second reef, which would expose the suspect repair, and the fourth reef that suited really heavy breezes. It was quite unnerving to be worrying constantly about breaking sails, but with no spares it was better to be prudent and carry on at a steady, if uninspiring, pace.

The highlight of my day was always when I received a message from Cindy. She would update me on things at home, such as 'Vance was stung by a bee'. It was strange to be in the same hemisphere and summer season while sailing in fog and often snow. Cindy would mention taking the children to the pool or spending a couple of hours at the beach. I was looking forward to getting home.

▲ *Telephoning home. Also seen is my single sideband radio, VHF radio and Furuno weatherfax.*

I found encouragement from the often huge number of birds that I would see. For most of the Southern Ocean legs I would constantly be in the company of various types of albatross, some of the largest seabirds in the world. And flocks of smaller birds of mixed species, numbering about twenty, would fly a circular path around the boat. The number of birds would always increase when within a couple of hundred miles of rocky outcrops such as the Crozets or Heard Island. On several occasions I observed flocks of what must have been thousands of small grey birds, a species of prion. It was delightful to see them out in all conditions, dipping and weaving across my course, surely wondering why the big bird with white wings never chirped back or joined them in their erratic flight.

The strong westerlies were not always reliable and I spent a couple of days in unexpected squally conditions with the wind blowing up to 40 knots in squalls with hardly any breeze between them. I had not expected the doldrums down here. Then a cold front came through, clearing the system out with gusts of over 53 knots and *Newcastle Australia* rocketed off on her way counting the miles to Bass Strait.

The front-running Class I boats were already through Bass Strait and tacking up the coast to Sydney. Christophe Auguin on *Sceta Calberson* was the first to arrive a few days before Christmas after an amazing passage of twenty-four days 23 hours. Jean Luc Van den Heede, exhausted from days of tacking within a mile of the shore, fell asleep and ended up on a beach 60 miles south of Sydney. *Vendée Enterprises* was towed off by a police launch and limped into Sydney for second place. *Kodak* and *True Blue* were fighting it out in sight of one another as they exited Bass Strait. They match raced for the last 500 miles arriving with only 2 hours between them. Steve Pettingill on *Hunters Child* arrived the same day to claim third place in Class I.

As the arriving skippers were enjoying Christmas pudding and celebrating with their families, race headquarters were once again shocked by the report that Isabelle's Emergency Position Indicating Radio Beacon (EPIRB) was activated, giving her position at 1000 miles south of Adelaide, South Australia. Isabelle had made a tremendous effort setting a jury rig and sailing 1200 miles to Kerguelen Island. Her sponsors in France had found and shipped to the island a 39 foot (11.9 m) mast that she stepped as a replacement for the remainder of the trip to Sydney where they would have a new mast waiting. Leaving Kerguelen Island she made great progress toward Tasmania. But now in an area of a deep low pressure cell her alarms sounded. With no response from her radio the authorities could only assume the worst.

None of the BOC fleet were near enough to render assistance, so the Australian military responded by sending aircraft into her vicinity. Within 24 hours of the EPIRB being activated she was spotted by an Air Force search plane. By signalling and dropping a radio to her it was determined that Isabelle was well but that her radical yacht had been overcome in huge breaking seas.

Ecureuil Poitou Charentes 2 had been rolled, totally destroying her stumpy jury rig and tearing the rudders from the boat. Her cabin blister, where she slept, ate and navigated, was crushed and actually broken from the deck leaving a gaping hole 16 feet square (5 m square). With the aft compartment flooded and water washing into her main cabin she had no way to save the boat. Forced into the forward sail locker, from where she set off the distress beacon, she huddled for the three days it took for the Australian Navy frigate *HMAS Darwin* to arrive. Once on station they were able to lift her off by helicopter. All the while the Air Force maintained a constant vigil, flying overhead in rotating shifts until she was safely in the hands of the Navy.

It was a credit to the people involved. The successful outcome resulted from the combined skills and co-operation of the Navy and Air Force working together with the Australian Maritime Rescue Co-ordination Centre in the national capital, Canberra.

▲ *During the Australian stopover the Royal Australian Air Force and Navy conducted a debriefing session on the effectiveness of the rescue operation of Isabelle Autissier. Isabelle, Mark Schrader and myself are here looking at the position where Isabelle's EPIRB was activated*   STEVE NEBAUER, A BEAR IMAGE

Two days after Christmas the seas became very rough. As I closed the entrance to Bass Strait the waves started to heap up in the shallower coastal waters. My first sight of land was at 0245 on 27 December after one month at sea. I could see the silhouette of Black Pyramid, a 240 foot (73 m) high rock marking the south-west entrance of the famous Strait. Tasmania was only 20 miles off my starboard side. I felt as though I had come home.

The transition was almost immediate as I sailed out of the Southern Ocean and into the Strait—the sky cleared and visibility improved dramatically, with my first sight of stars in what seemed like forever. The Southern Ocean is so consistently grey that after a few weeks it becomes normal and you forget how incredibly beautiful it is to see a brilliant clear starry night.

From Black Pyramid to Cape Howe on the north-eastern corner of Bass Strait on the Australian mainland it is about 300 miles through the 80 to 100 mile wide Strait that separates Tasmania from the rest of Australia. I found myself in favorable conditions as I headed to clear the Kent Group islands, about halfway through the Strait. The breeze remained from the west and south-west and dropped off considerably to around 20 knots.

I was so close to home and with a favorable weather report I unreefed *Newcastle Australia*'s mainsail fully for the first time since it was damaged in the gale eighteen days before. The day was clear and sunny. It was unnecessary to wear my waterproof clothes on deck and I began to take off the layers of thermal clothing. My cocooned skin felt sensitive and the sun was like medicine, warming and drying my bones.

The trip through the Strait went well but the wind went light and started to flick around the compass at only 5 to 6 knots. Finally as I neared Deal Island in the Kent Group it headed me and, sailing as close to the wind as possible, I managed to sneak past the island, after which I had to tack and began to work my way toward Cape Howe 170 miles away.

The shallow water and the currents combined with a headwind and sea made for uncomfortable sailing. After weeks of running before the westerly winds down south I was unaccustomed to the motion and the regular thump and banging as *Newcastle Australia* slammed into the short Bass Strait chop. Sydney suddenly seemed a long way away.

Niah Vaughan had entered Bass Strait about 24 hours after me. I had a reasonable lead but not enough to feel comfortable with. I could not relax and continued to sail hard, not prepared to lose any distance to him. There was a front forecast for later in the day that should bring with it strong southerly winds. A classic 'southerly buster' was brewing and I hoped it might take me all the way home.

The north-easterly wind persisted all day but on my western horizon could be seen a distinct band of cloud moving against the wind rapidly in my direction. As the cloud approached, strong wind warnings were broadcast for the area but they seemed overstated, with the sun shining and the clear blue sky overhead. It was not long before the band of cloud took on a more ominous look and I could see it clearly moving toward me. It appeared to

▲ *The roll cloud that brought me 50 knots of wind in Bass Strait*

not be very high and all I could see was a tight roll of cloud that stretched from horizon to horizon.

The wind was still from the north-east as the cloud bank moved directly above me and I could look up into this awesome sight to see the violence as the cloud twisted and rolled inside itself. I quickly reefed the sails to the fourth reef and rolled the genoa away, curious to see how this would go. Instantly the wind changed from the north-east to the south-west. Initially it blew at about 35 knots and strangely as the cloud moved over me the wind dropped off to about 15 knots. I thought it weird but bluffed by the blue sky and keen to use the favorable wind I shook the reefs out, only to have the wind come in stronger, requiring me to put the reefs in urgently again.

The boat shot off with the mainsail flogging violently as I reefed it again to the fourth reef point. The wind continued to build and within a few minutes my wind instruments were reading 55 knots. *Newcastle Australia* took off at 13 knots and then 17 knots bursting up to 20 knots. The motion and the noise were indescribable as we crashed through the short steep 6 foot (1.8 m) chop that was still coming from the north-east. The wind and sea were at odds and I had to hand-steer, feeling as though the boat would be torn apart.

As the second blast showed no signs of letting up, by nightfall I had stripped the boat of the mainsail and carried on under the blade jib. The seas gradually turned to come from the direction of the wind but had built and remained amazingly rough and confused. *Newcastle Australia* would surf down the closely spaced waves, slamming into the back of another. Sheets of spray would shoot high into the air with the inside of the boat sounding like an oil drum bouncing down a hill.

The gale continued at 35 to 40 knots for the next 14 hours, providing me with a rough and exhilarating ride through the night. To make matters worse, after all the weeks and miles of sailing in the uncongested Southern Ocean, I had to remain vigilant and continually be on a lookout for ships. I also had to alter course to clear the New Zealand Star Bank, a shallow patch marked on the chart as 'breaking in heavy weather'. At 0600 hours I spoke to the lighthouse keeper on Gabo Island and then shortly after rounded Cape Howe and was clear of the notorious Bass Strait.

It was Thursday, 29 December and I had been at sea for almost thirty-four days. The wind was down to 30 knots as I turned north for the last 220 miles to Sydney. Sheltered by the lee of the Australian continent the swell immediately flattened out and I began to run fast up familiar coast. If the wind held I could be in Sydney within 24 hours.

The Australian East Coast Current runs in a southerly direction at various rates throughout the year. This makes it difficult for a yacht to make good progress in a northerly direction against the current, especially in summer when the prevailing wind is from the north-east. There are two schools of thought for a northerly passage. One being to sail far offshore beyond the limit of the current. Two, the most common, is to hug the coast and beat uphill within a mile of the beach inside the edge of the stream. I opted for number two and was making great progress with the favorable south-westerly that had caused so much discomfort and noise during the night. In the flat seas *Newcastle Australia* sped for home.

I called BOC control in Sydney and gave my ETA as 0900 the following morning. I was praying that the wind would hold. While down below fixing my breakfast I suddenly heard a mighty roar of engines screaming past. I poked my head out of the hatch to see a small single-engine aircraft flash past, not much higher than the top of my 72 foot (22 m) mast. There was an arm out the window waving excitedly and I could actually hear a garbled shout from the passenger.

It turned out that my oldest brother Stephen was so excited by my pending arrival that he had hired a plane and flown out to welcome me back to Australia. Camping in his car on the beach and tracking me by telephone calls and radio reports he had waited until I closed the coast and, with the pilot ready, had flown out for a unique view of *Newcastle Australia*. Steve is a professional photographer based in Canberra and he was keen to capture an image of the boat in its element. After buzzing me for over an hour he returned to ground and watched me for a couple of hours from shore, driving first from one headland to another. He later said that it had a profound effect on him to see me in the process of achieving what I had set out to do.

▶ *Newcastle Australia* sailing *off Green Cape taken from a single-engine aircraft by my brother* STEVE NEBAUER, A BEAR IMAGE

Not long after Steve's noisy welcome the wind went into a typical New South Wales pattern and began to back into the south-east and east—classic symptoms presaging a wind shift to the north-east. Gradually it swung and eased right off for most of the day, although into the night I was able to

◄

Newcastle Australia *surfing along the New South Wales coast with four reefs in the mainsail and a jib*
STEVE NEBAUER, A BEAR IMAGE

lay my course, occasionally grinding in the sails until I was close-hauled on a starboard tack.

At 2000 hours that night the wind died altogether and I realised that my ETA was blown out the window. I was happy to have made it closer to home before losing the wind but still it was frustrating to be so close and yet so far from the finish. I had a 2 knot current against me and no wind. Niah remained in wind as he was exiting Bass Strait and I was all too aware of the slim lead I had over him on this leg. All night I was up chasing every puff of wind. It felt as though I was inching my way up the coast.

Dawn found me drifting off Point Perpendicular with only 70 miles to go. With the constant tacking and adverse current I actually logged twice that distance before making Sydney. Finally at 1100 hours the breeze started to gently blow from the north and then settled in at 15 knots from the north-east. Sydney was dead to windward as I continued to tack my way up the shoreline. In an effort to stay inside the south-flowing current I would sail in until a few hundred feet from the beach and then tack out for about 2 miles or 13 minutes. I would then transfer my water ballast over, ready for the new tack, and once again head in toward the beach. This went on hour after hour.

The north-easterly steadily built to 21 knots true wind strength and it was putting a lot of pressure on my damaged mainsail but I needed all the power I could get. I was amazed that the sail held up. It was fantastic to pass the coastal towns and every hour draw closer to the finish line inside Sydney heads.

Cindy and my family had driven to Sydney to meet me based on my original ETA of Friday morning. My parents were there and my sisters and their families had come down from country New South Wales. Media from our home town of Newcastle travelled down for the scoop. Friends from home had heard and there was a collection of over fifty friends and relatives waiting on the docks only to be disappointed when told that I had been becalmed all night and that I may not arrive till the morrow.

I really felt under the gun when I found out about the keen group but there was nothing I could do but keep on going as I was. *Newcastle Australia* was sailing close-hauled hard on the wind at a steady 9.3 knots, although with the current and loss due to tacking angles I was closing the gap at about 7 knots. I took time out to enjoy the view. The coastal towns were merging into the loom of the lights of Sydney and it was a wonderful sight.

Now that I was back it seemed like no time since I had left Australia and had sailed 27 000 miles around the world. But I was only halfway through the BOC Challenge and I still had a long way to go before my job was finished.

I began to check in with Mark Schrader at BOC control every couple of hours updating my position and ETA. At 0300 hours on Saturday I could see a gap in the shore lights indicating the entrance to Sydney Harbour and, on a dying breeze, turned *Newcastle Australia* in. Out of the confusion of all the city lights, the navigation lights of a large inflatable dinghy appeared. It was Mark and Herb from BOC control, and Cindy and my brother Mick were on board. There were calls across the water of congratulations and welcome home.

I was not quite finished yet and drifted the last few hundred feet at a gentle pace. Another motor boat appeared crowded with my parents, my sisters and brother with their children all waving and calling out greetings over the water. The siren sounded at 0400 hours signalling my finish as I slipped across the line. There were whistles and cheers—it was a fabulous moment.

Cindy and Mick climbed aboard as did Mark and Herb in their official capacities with BOC and it was great to see everyone. A moment later Annie and Vance were passed up to me from a dinghy. I handed the wheel to Mark and sat on deck holding my children for the tow up the harbor. The quiet harbor was beautiful as we were towed past the Opera House and under the famous Harbour Bridge.

Finally we tied *Newcastle Australia* to a berth at the City West marina complex near Darling Harbour. I was overwhelmed again at the reception— David and Caroline Adams were there and more friends and relatives who had stayed up all night to greet me. After a time of questions from media and well-wishers I was able to slip off with Cindy and the children. I had made it. I had completed a circumnavigation and had arrived in third place after thirty-four days 4 hours. It was good to be home.

CHAPTER SIX

Australian stopover

It FELT strange to be back in our cottage by the shore of Lake Macquarie near Newcastle. I had arrived on New Year's Eve and, with the restart for leg three set for 29 January, I looked forward to having some time off with Cindy and the children. However, that was not to be the case.

From the first morning home we were inundated with telephone calls. The telephone started to ring at 0700 hours and rang over forty times before 1100 hours—why didn't I take it off the hook? After a while we stopped answering it but by lunchtime I had done several radio and newspaper interviews and two film crews had come to make reports. Annie and Vance got sick of all the fuss and blatantly refused to perform for the cameras. It would have been preferable to have sent them away until we had had a break but we co-operated because all our sponsors and a large number of community supporters were interested in hearing my tale. It was necessary but we found it very draining.

A month ashore seemed to be a long time and Cindy and I planned to spend some time together with Annie and Vance. However, I had accrued a list of jobs to be done while in port. There were sails to be mended and the generator had an oil leak. I also wanted the electrical system checked but due to overlaps in people's schedules it turned out that some things would be overlooked. My brother Mick also took five weeks off work so that he could help out. Because *Newcastle Australia* was due to be in her home port for one week in the middle of the stopover we had two deadlines. The first was to have the majority of the repairs done before the sail from Sydney to Newcastle to participate in the promotional weekend that my

65

▲ *When I arrived in Sydney we were inundated by the media*
STEVE NEBAUER, A BEAR IMAGE

home city had organized. The second was for the real thing, the restart and the trip to the infamous Cape Horn.

Being back in my home town brought back memories of the lead up to the race. Our sponsorship campaign for the BOC Challenge had overwhelmed our lives for the three years prior to the start of the race. Cindy and I had begun the campaign in the middle of 1991, having just returned to Australia after a four and a half year voyage around the Pacific.

In 1987 we had sailed our 25 foot (7.6 m) yacht, *Deus Regit II*, from Newcastle, east and north across the Pacific Ocean via New Zealand, French Polynesia and Hawaii over a six month period to British Columbia in Canada. Here we were enrolled in a Bible college. We lived in Canada for two years and Annie was born on Vancouver Island a few weeks before we left to sail south to Mexico in 1989, where we were based for fourteen months, working on charter yachts and delivering yachts up to 80 feet (24 m). Eventually, having decided to commit to the BOC Challenge, we headed *Deus Regit II* west out of Acapulco for the four month passage back home to Newcastle via the Marquesas, Tahiti, Cook Islands and Tonga. As Cindy was six months pregnant, she flew home from the Marquesas and I sailed 5000 miles single-handed back home.

▲ *With Cindy and Annie, who is five days old, beside our yacht* Deus Regit II *(on our right) in Maple Bay, Vancouver Island*

It had been a dream of mine since an eight-year-old to sail around the world by myself. Who knows what inspired me but from such an early age all my attention was focused on learning to sail so that one day I could head off. I am sure that originally I was motivated by a degree of escapism and a desire to buck the system. I found it difficult to concentrate at school, finding most of what I was taught irrelevant to the ocean voyaging lifestyle that I was anticipating. Little did I realize that an education would help speed up my escape.

Surviving school with my dreams intact, at the age of sixteen I joined a sloop on a trip to New Zealand via Hobart. We spent 30 hours in a cyclone with 80-knot winds and 45 foot (13.7 m) seas. I took it in my stride thinking that 'wet and miserable' must be part of the deal and I have kept going back to the sea ever since. I worked in various fields, often far from the sea, to earn enough money for my own early voyaging. I launched my first cruising yacht when I was twenty-one and the following year bought the hull and deck of the boat that was to be my home for five years and, after fitting her out, met and married Cindy.

Deus Regit II was launched in November 1986 near Newcastle, my home port and the city where Cindy grew up. It is a fantastic area with countless attributes. Historically, it is the birthplace of Australia's industry, with the first export from Australia leaving from this port. The heart of this progressive city is surrounded by beaches and a beautiful coastline. There are bays and coastal lakes with sheltered anchorages, making up one of the best cruising grounds I have seen around the world. Further inland the landscape changes from rich alluvial flats to quality wine-growing areas and world-renowned horse- and cattle-breeding districts.

▲ *Newcastle has countless attributes, including beautiful beaches and waterways*

While we were cruising, we always loved to tell people who enquired about where we were from about the Newcastle region and encourage them to head out and see it for themselves. So when the time came and I felt I had the experience to take on the BOC Challenge, it was our first inclination to head back home and put together a regional-based project with local sponsors. The plan was that if we could not get one big sponsor, why not have many smaller sponsors working as a co-operative to promote the region.

We met with some early encouragement for the 'big dream' and also much antagonism toward the project. Many people forecasted that it would never get off the ground. However, we were deadly serious about the task. Cindy and I believe that it is God who inspires and motivates us to live our lives and we were confident that if we started this in faith we would be able to finish it in faith.

An early break came when, at a function, an engineer named Rob Barker introduced himself. Rob had experience in business management and at running large construction projects. He was a stickler for details and, although he had never sailed, he saw involvement in our project as a challenge and casually offered to help. This casual offer turned into a three-year epic of highs and lows, late nights and countless planning meetings.

As the campaign grew Rob took much time off from his own business to concentrate on our project. We had access to his office, staff and equipment, with his staff typing hundreds of proposals for us and keeping our newsletter and correspondence up to date. We greatly valued his input. John Griffiths and Bruce Robertson, two other invaluable friends, also joined our team. They brought with them their own particular skills and expertise, contributing much towards the continuation of the project.

When we began our campaign, we presented the idea to several business people in the area who became early supporters and stuck with us through the hard campaign process. We enlisted the support of the then Lord Mayor of Newcastle, John McNaughton, who became our patron. With his endorsement we had credibility and began to seek sponsorship avidly. We formed a supporters' group with membership fees of $A1000 and also knocked on every corporate door in the area. 'The BOC what . . . ?' would often be the initial response but, on consideration, people became captivated by the idea.

We had hoped to find one or two big corporations that would back us but the concept was too unconventional. They liked what we were doing and could see the value in it but the concept was so new that many people found it hard to commit serious cash to the project. However, the support group grew gradually to more than one hundred members and we found six major sponsors that were keen to work with us.

Through all this Cindy was marvellous. She went to every meeting and organized receptions, breakfast meetings and fundraising dinners. She wrote hundreds of proposals and was the media representative when I was unavailable. She designed and marketed the T-shirts as well as looked after our children.

We settled on a design by David Lyons and, after speaking with several boatbuilders, we settled on Jarkan Yacht Builders. The principal, Kanga Birtles, had competed in the 1990–91 BOC Challenge and was prepared to work with us even before we had any significant sponsors in place. His price was very competitive and we got on well so it was an easy decision. As the building of the boat progressed and money was a struggle, Kanga ran the gauntlet and kept on building, trusting that we would find enough money.

In April 1994, with time running out, and only ten weeks before I was due to leave Australia, we approached the Newcastle City Council with a proposal that they consolidate the already strong regional support by underwriting a portion of the budget. This would at least ensure that the

▲ *With Kanga Birtles during the building of* Newcastle Australia
STEVE NEBAUER, A BEAR IMAGE

boat would be finished and perhaps draw a commitment from one of the potential major sponsors we had been dealing with. After a unanimous vote the Council went with us on the loan and we made every conceivable effort, launching the boat in early June.

I was scheduled to leave for Charleston, South Carolina, on 10 June but after sorting everything out I was unable to leave until 25 June. Thus, I had ten weeks to complete the 11 400 mile delivery. To qualify for the BOC Challenge I sailed 4000 miles single-handed to Tahiti, where Cindy then joined me for the remaining approximately 8000 miles, via the Panama Canal. We arrived at Charleston at noon on 7 September, 1.5 hours before the scrutinizing deadline when boats are checked to ensure they meet race rules.

And here I was now, halfway through the race with escalated community interest and support as they watched the progress of the race. Schools were involved through the BOC Oceanwatch program, a worldwide learning program that taught geography, navigation and life skills through following

▲ *Busy building* Newcastle Australia *in May 1994*   STEVE NEBAUER, A BEAR
IMAGE

▲ *Proud volunteers: Peter Routley, Glenn Currington and Bruce Jones*

◀

Newcastle Australia *in the*
Panama Canal taken from
the container vessel
Clifford Maersk
MIKKEL BIRGER HANSEN

the race, and the newspapers, and radio and television stations were running weekly updates for their audiences who were apparently keen for any news of the race.

After the race start in Charleston, and at the instigation of Bill Grant, the Newcastle City General Manager, a committee was formed to organize a major fundraising event during the Australian stopover. This was separate from our own initiatives and would provide a unique and exciting promotion for Newcastle, while also paying some bills to help keep me racing.

The committee worked for weeks to design an event they called The Great Race, in which all forms of transport—aircraft, Harley Davidsons, cars, trains, buses and helicopters—would race the yacht *Newcastle Australia* from Sydney to Newcastle. It would be a staggered start to ensure that all the entries converged at the same time at the magnificent park that lined the harbor foreshore. The plan was to emphasize the easy access to the region and the fact that the city of Newcastle is a worthwhile tourist or business destination.

It was incredible to sail home and see how much effort had gone into the program. There was a cocktail party on board the warship *HMAS Newcastle* and over 10 000 people were gathered on the waterfront as we sailed in, with public concerts and a regatta on the harbor.

► *Newcastle Australia sailing on Newcastle Harbour during the Australian stopover* STEVE NEBAUER, A BEAR IMAGE

Jimroda II and *Novell South Africa* sailed up with us and most of the BOC sailors and entourage travelled up for the weekend as guests of the city. Josh and Laura Hall even flew out for the festivities as guests of the city of Newcastle. It was fantastic to realize that the whole city had taken ownership of the campaign. We were still far from meeting our budget but, as far as community involvement went, our campaign was on top.

Meanwhile, such a hectic schedule—working on the boat, commuting to Sydney each day, seeing family and friends, and all the public appearances and late nights—began to take its toll on me. I became exhausted and run down and picked up a flu bug that was to knock me flat for the last week of preparations. I had a high fever during a meeting with one of my Sydney sponsors, who must have thought me to be the most unsociable and dreariest sailor in the world.

Newcastle Australia was due to be delivered back to Sydney one week before the restart. A friend of mine, Stephen Chapman, one of only a few people that I would trust with the boat, had offered to deliver her back so that I could have a day with Cindy and the children. The only day he was available to make the trip dawned grey and ugly, with gale-force southerly winds beating on the front of our house.

It was a miserable day for the trip south down the coast with a 35 to 40 knot headwind and rough seas against them. Chapo and his crew were beaten up pretty severely. To add to their misery the mainsail split at the second reef point in exactly the same way it had for me at the third reef point during the leg from Cape Town. The sail had had enough—by now it had been around the world and I had sailed over 30 000 miles with it. I lost confidence in it for the next leg to Uruguay via Cape Horn and had no choice but to condemn it. We did not have the luxury of spare sails and had planned to use the sail all the way but now we were forced to order a new one.

With only four days to make and fit the new mainsail, and with our sailmaker being unavailable and having to find someone else to do it, I called Colin Rogers, managing director of my major sponsor, NIB Health Funds, while he was away on holidays. Fortunately, he offered to pay for the replacement.

However, I was still out of action with the flu and so my brother Mick relentlessly carried on with the work on board. Jim and Ann Cate, some American friends from our cruising days, were in town on their boat *Insatiable* and offered to help. Serge Viviand, Isabelle Autissier's shore crew, also spent a couple of days chipping away at the list. My parents were also fantastic, spending much of the time during this stopover on the dock selling promotional T-shirts to raise more funds.

Suddenly it was the eve of my departure. A month had sped past and still Cindy and I had only managed to have one uninterrupted night away with Annie and Vance. I felt guilty about that but I hoped that they understood.

Once again it was the presentation night for the previous leg, which was also a big event. Christophe Auguin on *Sceta Calberson* won the Class I section and David Adams on *True Blue* won Class II. This time my family and many of our sponsors and supporters were able to come down to Sydney for the night. Most were staying overnight as we had arranged for a motor boat to take them out to see the restart. Everyone was excited and in a real party mood. However, I just wanted to take some Panadol and go to sleep.

CHAPTER SEVEN

To Bluff for repairs

THE leg three restart at noon on Sunday, 29 January turned out to be an absolutely perfect Sydney summer day. With the wind blowing at about 3 knots from the east the start was a bit of a muddle as the fleet of thirteen boats (Harry Mitchell started a day late) drifted around in the lee of North Head. A recently launched replica of Captain Cook's bark, *Endeavour*, was used as the start boat. It made an impressive sight and I wondered what it would be like to sail to Cape Horn in her.

David Adams showed off for his home town by being first across the line. As I crossed the line the wind picked up to about 8 to 10 knots. *Newcastle Australia* heeled with the pressure and started to power ahead. I was still as sick as a dog with the flu and found it difficult to summon up the energy to even return the friendly waves from the spectators motoring past. However, as a huge catamaran ferry with all of the shore crew aboard drew up alongside I laughed and probably blushed. There was Cindy on the foredeck behind a big yellow banner with 'Cindy loves Alan' written across it in black. I certainly managed an enthusiastic wave for her.

Leg three is the longest leg of the race. We had to sail over 7200 miles before reaching Punta del Este in Uruguay. Ahead lay weeks of sailing deep in the Southern Ocean. First I would head south below New Zealand and then turn and run east across the Pacific Ocean to Cape Horn. Much of the fleet would sail in waters beyond 60 degrees south. We could look forward to ice and days of gale-force winds before rounding Cape Horn and changing course to head up into the Atlantic Ocean.

For the first 35 hours out of Sydney there was hardly any wind and it was extremely hot. I was frustrated to notice that two sail battens in my new mainsail had broken, poking through the sail as it hung limp during the calm. During the second day a breeze developed from the north-east and I made some good miles. I was sailing in sight of *Novell South Africa*, *Kodak*, *Thursday's Child* and *Jimroda II*. However, the breeze steadily increased as it shifted through to the south-west and the following morning we had a gale from the south-south-west. The gale continued to build and to swing, blowing from the south and south-east—steady 40 to 50 knots right on the nose! Soon there were reports of 70-knot winds, blown sails and boats being knocked down. This was the Tasman Sea at its best!

Minoru on *Shuten-Dohji II* had to head into Port Kembla on the New South Wales south coast for repairs to his satellite communicator but was soon underway again. Then Nigel on *Skycatcher* had problems with his rudder bearings, which had seized, and his mainsail, which had blown out, forcing him to make for Ulladulla, also on the south coast. With his destroyed mainsail taking at least a week to replace and needing to haul *Skycatcher* out of the water to change the rudder bearings, he felt that he would be foolhardy to continue so far behind the psychological safety net provided by the fleet. He sadly decided to withdraw, leaving only thirteen competitors in the race.

The fleet continued to be battered by strong southerlies. Jean Luc on *Vendée Enterprises*, who was in the lead, faxed headquarters describing the rough sea as 'starting to be rude'.

On the fifth day out I was alarmed to notice that while I was charging the generator the alternators were only producing a very low output. I checked the system but was unable to find anything obviously wrong. However, the following morning when I ran the generator to charge my batteries I discovered, to my disgust, that neither of the alternators were working at all. During the stopover in Sydney a battery boost block had been installed to increase the output of the alternators while charging. I thought that this may have caused some interference but after spending most of the day experimenting with different wiring combinations and refitting some connections I found no improvement. Once again I had to admit defeat to the unreliability of my charging system and stop for repairs.

This was a huge blow for me psychologically. I had been looking forward to a trouble-free passage on this leg. My boat was as fast as the other new 50 foot (15.2 m) yachts—*True Blue* and *Kodak*. I knew that I lacked some of the experience of David Adams, a veteran of the 1990–91 BOC Challenge, and Giovanni Soldini had previously raced a 50 foot (15.2 m) boat in the Atlantic Ocean. I was determined to stay with them on this leg. So far I had been within 30 to 60 miles behind the front-runners of Class II. I was happy with third place and, due to my flu and the rough conditions, I had been sailing cautiously, not pushing too hard so as to reduce the risk of breaking something so early in this leg of the race.

And now for the second time I was without power. *Newcastle Australia* was totally dependant on electricity to run the three autopilots as well as the computers and other electrical systems on board. I could have carried on successfully without my radar or the satellite navigation system (GPS) but I could not have sailed competitively for a month in freezing Southern Ocean conditions if I had to hand-steer. To be exposed every day to the merciless cold because I had no autopilots would have been futile. I felt crushed and humiliated.

The closest port to me where I would be able to fix the alternators was Bluff, a town located at the very bottom of the South Island, New Zealand, 300 miles to my south-east. I notified race control that I would be diverting and that I had charts of the area. To get to Bluff would mean a significant detour. I first had to make landfall near Puysegur Point at the western end of Foveaux Strait. The wind had been on the nose all the way across the Tasman Sea at gale or near-gale force and, on making the Strait, it continued to head me, clocking around to the east.

Once into Foveaux Strait I had to beat 90 miles up into Bluff. For once, however, the headwinds did me a favor. I had installed a wind-driven generator in Sydney and was keen to use it during this leg as a means to supplement my diesel generator. It consisted of a fan that spun in the breeze, driving a small electric generator. It provided a limited amount of power but not enough to meet the demands that I required. It was most efficient with the wind against me, when the combination of the boat's forward motion and the wind speed increased the apparent breeze spinning the fan. It would not have helped much in conditions when I was sailing fast off the breeze as the decreased apparent wind on the fan rendered it almost useless. However, for the beat into Bluff it generated enough power to supplement my low batteries and added to the safety of my landfall because I could use my electronic navigation equipment and I did not have to hand-steer.

David Scully on *Coyote* was also en route to Bluff because he had blown out his mainsail in the strong Tasman Sea gales. As I cleared Puysegur Point and began the windward beat along the coast to Bluff, David was also closing the coast. He had been almost level with Bluff but several hundred miles west at the time that he had diverted for repairs. Later in the day we were swapping tacks in sight of each other. David had no detailed charts of the area and periodically he would relay his position to me. I would then plot him on my chart and calculate the course for him to steer for the next

▲ *David Scully's* Coyote   BILLY BLACK/BOC

tack so that he would be clear of obstructions as he threaded his way among the reefs and small islands along the coast.

At 2000 hours that night I was pleased to hear the voice of my good friend Martin Picard hailing me on the VHF radio. Martin, on hearing of my problems and diversion to Bluff, had called Cindy offering to help. He ended up flying to Christchurch, New Zealand, and making his way down to Bluff. On arrival he began to organize the repairs. It was a godsend that he had come.

Unfortunately, my arrival in Bluff was on a public holiday weekend. However, before he had left Australia, Martin and Cindy had found an electrician familiar with my brand of alternators. Now ashore at Bluff, Martin had primed the technician he had organized as to the urgency of our situation and also liaised with the harbor pilots to tow *Coyote* and *Newcastle Australia* in once we were off the harbor entrance. He had everything under control, which took some of the worry from me. His help and organization saved both of us from losing a huge amount of time out of the race.

All through our campaign and during the race around the world I was amazed by the kindness and helpfulness of so many people. People were so intrigued and curious about our sailing lifestyle and the idea of a solo race around the world that they offered their time or help in many different ways. Often their motivation was, apart from a generous attitude, a way to be involved in an adventure that so few people have been able to share in. Most people are more than happy only to hear about a trip like this, with only a relative few actually wanting to do it. Martin's efforts and encouragement are a classic example of how friends, family and strangers contributed to make sure that my race happened.

Bluff had been a port of call for other yachts in previous BOC Challenges. During the 1986–87 race Harry Mitchell, competing in a different boat to *Henry Hornblower*, had headed into Bluff for repairs to his boat after it was rolled and damaged during a storm similar to what the fleet had been experiencing all week in the Tasman Sea. Unfortunately, he had had no charts of the Bluff area and, after making a safe landfall and negotiating Foveaux Strait during a gale, had been given incorrect information by a radio operator on shore and was blown up onto a beach just to the east of Bluff Harbour. The boat was later refloated but it put an end to Harry's 1986–87 BOC aspirations.

As I neared Bluff I was very conscious of Harry's experience and was determined not to repeat it. Sailing close inshore meant I could not sleep for the last 24 hours of the approach. I had to remain vigilant and maintain an accurate and regular check of my position.

The wind was blustery and it was very bumpy sailing against wind and current. David Scully had overtaken me during the night and picked up the tow line at 0315 hours. Fortunately for us the pilot crew were on duty at this hour as they were on their way back from having taken a large ship out to sea. I arrived shortly after David and hove-to, waiting for the pilot boat to return for me. It was with relief that I came alongside *Coyote*, which was tied to a vacant wharf in the big ship terminal. Martin was on the dock to take my lines and we headed off for some breakfast and a shower before the technician arrived.

The technician turned out to be the regional dealer for the Australian-made alternators that I had on board. He made some preliminary checks and took the suspect units away for a more thorough inspection. He had to make a number of round trips of about 60 minutes each to his workshop and back before determining that the voltage regulators used to control the amount of current produced were burnt out. The next step was to determine exactly what was causing the problem. After checking every wire and connection in the system it became apparent that a short circuit had developed, causing both regulators to burn out.

He also recommended replacing the alternator switches that had been the problem on leg two as they appeared to be of inferior quality. Not wanting to risk any further trouble I, of course, agreed. This meant another trip to his workshop for some guaranteed-to-be-excellent switches. On return he installed them and tidied up some wiring, and then checked and rechecked everything several times before pronouncing the electrical system cured.

Meanwhile I had been working on deck trying to repair the mainsail and its battens, five of the six battens having now broken and ripped through the sail at the end of their pockets near the luff. The battens were undersized and kept poking out of their pockets, catching on everything in sight. This made it very difficult in heavy weather to reef and unreef the mainsail as the battens would often catch in the rigging or spreaders so that the sail would not go up or down, forcing me on several occasions to shinny up the mast to clear the trouble.

There was no sailmaker in the area but an old fellow on the dock offered to help me. We sewed heavy pieces of webbing on the end of the batten pockets in an effort to reinforce the damaged parts of the sail. The broken battens were now much shorter than they needed to be and I had to jam them into the luff as far as possible, clamping them there and then tightly handstitching them in place at the back end so that they would not slide forward and begin poking through the luff again. When hoisted the ten-day-old sail looked very untidy at the leech, the curved area at the back of the sail, which was now unsupported by the battens because their lengths were not the full width of the sail. The very back edge of the sail flapped around instead of setting nicely. I could do nothing about the weakness of the actual battens but they seemed as if they would be less of a problem with some of the compression loads taken off the unsupported leech.

It was now after dusk and the end of the pilot boat crew's shift as the repairs were being finished. With no ship movements scheduled they were going off watch for the night. Brent and Ian, the co-skippers of the pilot boat, promised to be back first thing in the morning to tow me out. It meant another night ashore but at least I could continue tidying up without rushing. With not a breath of wind and an adverse current, one of the worst combinations for sailing close inshore without an engine, I did not feel too bad about having to wait until the morning for a tow out of the harbor. It would have been unwise to sit a mile from the harbor mouth with no wind, drifting in the current so close to land and shoals and unable to maneuver the boat or sleep.

Waking early the following morning, I had a quick breakfast with Martin and went to meet the pilot boat for the 2 mile tow out to sea. However, the conditions were the same as the previous evening—not even a ripple disturbed the slate-gray surface of the water. They cast me off and *Newcastle Australia* floated aimlessly. The pilot boat circled me and the crew and Martin waved a salute before heading back to shore to help David Scully exit. He had borrowed a mainsail from David Adams and had had it sent over from Australia. After working all night with the help of Dave Barnaby, the shore crew from *Hunters Child*, he had almost finished fitting the replacement sail.

Gradually, a gentle breeze came in from the east and the boat began to make way. For the first 20 miles I made a course to avoid some obscure rocks and small islands. As I drifted south along the coast of Stewart Island I snacked on pavlova, a rich meringue and cream dessert, which the wife of Ian, one of the pilot boat skippers, had made for me. I reflected on how much had been done and on how blessed I was to have such good friends. Martin had generously taken care of all the costs involved with no thought of recompense. Thanks seemed so inadequate.

CHAPTER EIGHT

Trouble brewing

WHEN I left Bluff this leg of the race was now nine days old. Once again I found myself far behind my rivals in Class II, although it was good to be underway again. David Scully had left Bluff at around noon and he too was excited to be moving again; he followed me south down the coast of Stewart Island. He always seemed so cheerful, even when things were not going his way. Like mine, his stop in Bluff was the second stop he had been forced to make to repair faulty gear.

We spoke on the radio and David casually informed me that at that moment his wife Veronique was in labor in a Paris hospital having their second child. I could not believe how cool he was. Most of the fleet waited in suspense until the following morning when we found out that she had given birth to a daughter—Blanca.

Cape Horn was about 3800 miles away, a distance that I should have been able to cover in seventeen to twenty days. I was keen to catch up as I was now placed fifth in Class II. After about five hours with the wind flicking from all directions, the breeze finally settled in from the south-west building up until it was blowing 25 knots. Typically it was wet, gray and drizzly. I was depressed by my loss of time with the stopover but gradually I established a routine and I was encouraged by sailing fast again into the Southern Ocean. Before long it seemed as though I had never stopped and I began to concentrate on sailing the boat as fast as I could.

In the first 8 hours from Bluff I only covered 35 miles but at the end of 24 hours I had sailed 212 miles out of Bluff. I had even moved up one place in the fleet by overtaking Robin Davie on *Cornwall*. Robin was sailing the oldest boat in the fleet for his second BOC Challenge. He was not here to win but sailed the older style 40 foot (12.2 m) yacht remarkably well, maintaining a consistent average speed that I am sure he was proud of. Even though *Cornwall* is smaller and expected to be slower than *Newcastle Australia*, it certainly was an encouragement to move ahead of another boat—I felt like I was racing again.

That evening I was surprised to see a ship off my starboard side. I spoke to the officer on watch by VHF radio and he told me the ship was the US tanker *Richard Jamieson* en route to New Zealand from McMurdo Base in Antarctica, which they had been supplying with fuel. I could hardly believe him when he said that there were over 1200 people in residence at the base during the summer months—suddenly the Southern Ocean began to feel crowded. It was exciting to speak to him so far from any normal shipping lanes but I thought that he sounded blasé, as if speaking to a person on a yacht below the fiftieth parallel was an everyday occurrence.

Not long after noon on my twelfth day out of Sydney I crossed the international dateline and entered the Western Hemisphere. I had to change my watch as I moved from one time zone to another and as I crossed the dateline I had Friday all over again. I was 3 hours ahead of Cindy at home in Australia but one day behind her.

The front-running boats were powering on ahead enjoying the fresh conditions. Christophe in the lead on *Sceta Calberson* must have been ecstatic to record the fastest day's run for the race—he logged over 350 miles for a 24-hour period. It was not long, also, before ice was sighted— Jean Luc on *Vendée Enterprises* was the first to report seeing a huge iceberg 4 miles long and 100 feet (30 m) high as he sped east at 13 knots—he was at 57.50 degrees south, 152.40 degrees west.

For the first few days out of Bluff I enjoyed suspiciously mild weather. I knew that this could not last for much longer. By day 15 I was in winds of near-gale force, the drizzly sky taking on an ominous look. With a dropping barometer the wind rapidly began to build out of the north-west. As I carried on averaging 10 knots it became obvious that soon the weather would get serious.

Later that night I could see stars poking through the swiftly scudding clouds. It was an incredibly clear and beautiful night—one to remember. However, it was crisp and cold on deck and the seas were very rough. I had closed to within 55 miles of *Jimroda II* and I was keen to press on, hoping to pass him as I carried the front forward to him. The wind oscillated between the north-west and the south-west creating a very confused cross-sea that threw *Newcastle Australia* around, often violently. Whatever happened to the majestic, rolling Southern Ocean swells I had come to see?

All through the night *Newcastle Australia* tore on with three reefs in the mainsail and a small jib set. The rough seas were harder on me and the boat than the strength of the storm-force winds. We were constantly thrown into one gapping trough after another. By daybreak the wind had settled at 60 knots. The barometer had dropped from 1020 millibars to 997 millibars since the previous morning. The seas were rough and huge, probably 40 feet (12.2 m).

I needed to reduce sail from the already deeply reefed mainsail. It took about an hour, with two battens breaking, for me to drag the sail down. The strength of the wind kept pressing the sail against the rigging, making it very difficult to lower the sail. Eventually, with my heart in my mouth, I had to turn *Newcastle Australia* around and head her up toward the wind and waves, so that by flogging the sail would shake free and slide down the track in the mast. Finally the mainsail was down and tied securely to the boom and with only the small jib set reefed to half its size we were still sailing at more than 10 knots—it seemed as though the wind and sea were out of control. By now the wind was screaming and gusting at over 60 knots.

I was making my way forward to raise the tiny storm jib when *Newcastle Australia* was picked up by a wave and thrown down onto her beam ends with the mast parallel to the turbulent water. Because I was on the leeward side of the boat I was immersed into the sea, my chest-high waterproof trousers and rubber sea boots filling with freezing cold sea water. Hanging on for dear life as the boat picked herself up and staggered to the top of the next crest, I thanked God that we had come through and that it was daylight. From the top of the crests I could see for miles in either direction—the sea was torn up into a mass of foaming, deep valleys. The sun reflecting off the dark pyramidal slopes seemed ironic.

After my dunking, I continued forward, soaking wet, to finish setting the storm jib. With the little sail set we still continued to fly. I went down below to change into dry clothes to try and ward off the numbing effect of the freezing water that had drenched me to the skin. The sun shone deceitfully through the cabin windows and it was strangely quiet inside after the fury on deck; but outside the wind and sea continued to roar unabated. The violent motion of the boat as it was thrown about made movement difficult as I dragged off my saturated garments and vigorously began to towel myself dry.

It was marvellous to slip into clean and dry thermal underwear and I felt snug in my new, bright red knee-length socks. I moved cautiously so as not to ruin them on the wet floor before I put my feet into my spare dry sea boots.

Suddenly a wave picked *Newcastle Australia* up, engulfing her in tons of water. I instantly knew that this was going to be bad. I stood, grabbing for a handrail above my head, while the boat slammed down onto her starboard side and rolled so that the mast was beyond the horizontal. Everything on the port side of the boat, including myself, crashed violently across the cabin. I ended up flying, falling backwards, landing with my head wedged under the deck-level mounted single sideband radio, my body following in a screaming heap into a longitudinal bulkhead near my chart table. The wind was knocked out of me as I was showered with the contents of my galley lockers.

Tin cans, bottled water, a kettle and frypan, a coffee mug, plates, knives, butter, onions and potatoes peppered onto me like a slow burst of machine-gun fire. My head and face were splattered with a thick, sticky substance. A jar of blackberry jam had collided with the cabin roof and exploded, showering everything with fragments of glass and the purple-black contents. These few seconds felt like minutes as the boat righted herself and screamed off down the face of another furious sea.

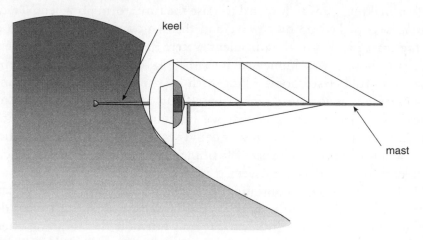

▲ *In a knockdown a vessel is knocked down to its beam ends and the mast is horizontal to the sea*

As *Newcastle Australia* became more upright I surveyed the chaos around and on top of me. Less than a minute before my cabin had been neatly arranged with everything in its place. Now there were wet charts stuck to the sides of the cabin and my calculator and navigation tools had, along with books and manuals, emptied themselves from my chart table. There was a pile of bedding, food and tools, like a load of gravel, dumped on the starboard side of the cabin.

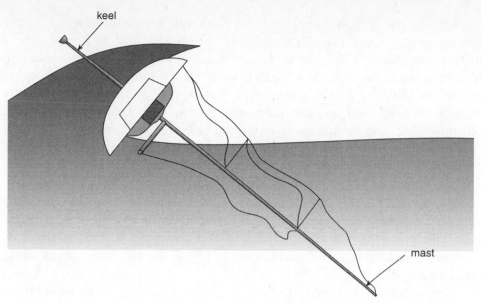

keel

mast

▲ *In a severe knockdown the mast is below the horizontal—not a very nice situation. This is usually caused by the state of the sea combined with the position of the boat relative to the sea at a particular time*

I staggered to my feet alarmed by a searing pain in my back—the area near my kidneys that had taken the impact of my fall felt pulverized. This had been my worst knockdown and I checked the boat for any signs of damage. My back and the whole right-hand side of my body ached intensely, severely restricting my movement, and I feared that some ribs may have been broken. On deck everything had held up well. I hand-steered for a while but the boat was hard-pressed and I was unable to steer any better than my autopilot owing to a lack of stamina as a result of the pain. I reset the autopilot and began to sort out the mess inside the boat. It was hard to know where to start.

I first grabbed any important books and fragile items that would be ruined by the salt water on the floor, or the dripping mess of jam that was spreading all over everything. I was very worried that I might be rolled again, so I remained in my wet-weather gear in case I should have to go on deck and began to restow my lockers. Whereas before they had been packed in some semblance of order relevant to the frequency of use, I now hastily stuffed them full and closed them off again as quickly as possible.

During the knockdown I had cut both my hands on glass from the broken jam jar and some 'unbreakable' plates that had shattered into a million fragments. I had put gloves on when I was hand-steering and had forgotten about the cuts. As I began to clean up the mess, blood was seeping out of the stitching on the gloves—the mess spread and there were bloody streaks over the floor and on charts, and mixing with jam and sea water. I felt miserable. Later when speaking on the radio to Niah on *Jimroda II*, my fierce rival, he became concerned about my condition when I described the pummelling I had received. He made sure to check in by radio at least once a day to see how I was.

Shortly after getting the boat in order another wave slammed *Newcastle Australia* over for a second time in as many hours. I had a better grip this time and the boat did not roll over as far as it did earlier in the day. However, many things still came crashing across the cabin and I was under rapid fire again.

Very gradually but surely the barometer began to rise as the storm front moved eastward. The conditions began to improve and the seas settled down enough for me to make more steady progress under the storm jib and blade jib. The wind dropped off to about 25 to 30 knots, which was light enough to hoist the reefed mainsail, but because of my back injury I was unable to raise the sail to push on hard. I had to be content to sail with reduced canvas, praying that my back would not be long in mending.

My Scheafer roller furling gear was a great bonus during this time because it was so easy to use. By hauling a line from the cockpit I had incremental control over the amount of jib I set for the conditions. With conventional hanked-on headsails it would have been very dangerous and difficult for me shuffling around on the foredeck dropping and raising sails with my aches and pains.

The barometer dropped again suddenly, making me nervous. I could exit my cabin reasonably quickly but because of the pain in my back it was very hard to get back inside the boat. Once inside, I had to lay flat on my bunk, drugged with Panadol Forte, and not move, which is hard to do on a boat at sea at the best of times. The last thing I wanted, with an injury and restricted movement, was another severe storm.

The next day, still with a very low barometer at 985 millibars, dawned clear and sunny, brightening my life for a few hours before turning moist and foggy. I saw several small dolphin-like creatures without fins frolicking in the swells and two small whales, which were probably pilot whales about 20 feet (6 m) long with a fin and a very blunt head. The wind started to back to the easterly quarter, requiring a huge effort from me to grind the mainsail up so that I could work to windward. It was extremely uncomfortable trying to progress into a headwind with a very confused and choppy westerly swell.

On the night of 16 February, while he was about 2500 miles from Cape Horn, Robin Davie on *Cornwall* was dismasted. I listened as he described to Niah and some of the other guys that he regularly spoke to on the radio about his mast breaking during a squall as he slept. The news rattled the fleet, with each one of us relating to how it would be, way down at these latitudes without the ability to sail well and not having maximum control of the boat. I spoke to Robin, hoping to sound encouraging, wishing him well.

During the 1986–87 BOC Challenge, a young Canadian skipper, John Hughes, lost his rig to the east of New Zealand and proceeded onto the Falkland Islands under a jury rig, becoming the first solo sailor to pass Cape Horn with a jury-rigged mast. Robin sounded cheerful on the radio, following Hughes' lead as he confidently improvised, creating an A-frame from two spinnaker poles lashed together at the top, from which he hung some small sails. About two days later he was underway, albeit not at his best speed but determined to keep on with the voyage. I admired him and was amazed at how positive he sounded, almost as if he was enjoying this new challenge.

On 23 February it was Niah Vaughan's fiftieth birthday. What a day it was—celebrated in typical Southern Ocean grandeur with big seas and big winds. I was sailing almost 100 miles south of Niah, poised to overtake him at last. I had been making some good miles and gaining on him after the slow progress of the previous week when I was forced to slow down because of my injuries. I thought with pleasure about what a great present it would make for him if I passed him on his birthday.

The big seas and big winds increased until evening when it was blowing a strong gale from the north-north-west at over 50 knots. I wondered how Niah was enjoying his birthday and whether he had this same weather further north. The seas were absolutely atrocious. My back was definitely on the mend after my last series of knockdowns, although still sore. However, the memories of my injury were vivid and by the look of the weather I could continue to expect a rough time ahead.

With the sea and wind raging I knew it was going to be another long night. I had to lower the mainsail once again completely and continue on under a jib only. It is hard to describe how hard and fast the breaking seas would hit and throw the boat around. There seemed to be an endless procession of violence—it was the type of night that makes you wonder what it is you have done wrong to end up here. Five times I was knocked down again so far that ice-cold jets of water would stream in through the top of my companionway washboards. The blasts of water would travel along the cabin ceiling and, as the boat righted herself, gallons of water would dump down over me and the navigation station, drenching everything in freezing sea water.

This was the first occasion that water actually entered the boat through a hatch opening and it thus caught me off guard. I was not expecting it to happen again but no sooner had I mopped up the navigation station than we were over again. My chart table was filled with water several times as was the alcove where I stored my computer, so vital for receiving weather analyses and the all-important fax link home. My laptop computer was thoroughly drowned as were several reference navigation books that had travelled with me for years—they were ruined.

▲ *View through my companionway showing typical Southern Ocean conditions. Note the drops of snow on the clear acrylic curtain*

It was the blackest night of my ocean voyaging life, with the winds far exceeding 70 knots. My heart was in my mouth as we raced on under bare poles, surfing at 12 knots, totally beyond any threshold of control. On deck it was impossible to steer or see anything—the air was solid water and I could not distinguish the sea from the sky. I could see neither the crests nor the troughs of the huge breaking waves. Notes from my log book sum it up as '*horrid*'.

Amid this tumult, I tuned in my single sideband radio for a pre-arranged call home to speak with Cindy and the children. It was a quick and somewhat bizarre contact. The reception was excellent and the voices of my family were booming in from the peace of our lounge room, more than 4000 miles away in Australia. Cindy was typically relaxed when I told her it was blowing 70 knots and gusting beyond 80 knots. She responded with a comment along the lines of 'it could be worse'. We prayed together, affirming our belief that God is in control of all things.

While I was experiencing this rough weather the front-running boats were making brilliant progress. Most of the Class I boats were now heading on a more northerly course after rounding Cape Horn. *True Blue* was around, for David's second doubling of the famous Cape. Giovanni on *Kodak* was not too far behind him, making Italian nautical history by becoming his nation's first solo sailor to round the five great capes of the Southern Ocean.

The next morning the weather began to settle down, relatively speaking. The wind dropped to below 50 knots and then 40 knots. It seemed almost pleasant compared with the previous night. However, an unruly swell was still running. Gradually the wind eased off until it was below gale force, and life returned to some form of normality.

It took some time for the big seas and the confusion that the storm had created to settle down but, with the wind now blowing at 20 to 30 knots, *Newcastle Australia* began to move steadily on course again. I could now put my head down for some much needed sleep.

Jury-rigged around Cape Horn

AFTER the storm that had given me a soaking my laptop computer failed to come back to life, even after hours of heating while the generator was running in an effort to dry it out. With the computer dead, my wonderful Standard-C was useless, resulting in me not being able to receive any weather or fleet position updates. It was also disappointing not being able to send notes home and I was frustrated at not knowing where I was in relation to the other boats, especially my arch rival Niah. He had been very quiet on the radio of late, so I was unsure if I was ahead of or behind him.

On the Saturday, 25 February, after my 'big blow' I was speaking to Arnie Taylor on *Thursday's Child*, who was about 300 miles east of me and had been slowed down after discovering a vertical crack in the base of his mast. Basically his mast was wearing away from the bottom up due to all the grinding and flexing during the continued rough weather. Arnie was concerned that if the wearing away worsened the mast would come down. For several days he had been pushing on with only headsails set to try and reduce some of the pressure on the damaged mast base.

Arnie was a real character and would often be the instigator, if not the butt, of some humor among the fleet. This morning, however, it was no joke as he cheerfully relayed the news that I had finally passed Niah during the previous night. I was pleased and excited to be back up to third place again with just over 800 miles to the Horn. My plan now became to be at least 100 miles in front of Niah as I doubled the famous Cape.

With the news of my gains I was enthused after being behind for so long. It was the twenty-eighth day of racing with about 2000 miles left before reaching Punta del Este, hopefully less than ten days sail away.

It was a different race for everyone. Christophe on *Sceta Calberson* was breaking records and had less than 200 miles to go. The same morning for the first time in many days I was able to hear Harry on *Henry Hornblower* and Minoru on *Shuten-Dohji II* check in on the radio schedule. The reception was weak but I listened to them reporting rough seas and a very low barometer. A massive depression was approaching them from the west.

Further east, my weather was milder although unstable, with squalls coming out of a drizzly wet sky. It was incredible how quickly the weather varied so far south, with no weather system remaining steady for more than a 10 to 12 hour period. I would have to gybe or tack to take advantage of the present conditions and at the same time consider possible changes that may take place over the next few days. It was critical to pay attention so that I would not be caught on the wrong side of a weather system. The Southern Ocean was a demanding but fascinating place to be.

After a rather frustrating overnight period, with the winds becoming very light and backing and veering countless times, Sunday 26 February dawned still and gray. I always found it unnerving to have light winds deep in the Southern Ocean—it seemed wrong to be drifting around when in an area notorious for dramatic gales and huge seas. Gradually the breeze came in whispers from the south and flicked around before settling in from the west.

With the westerly breeze filling in, the horizon behind me brightened. A band of blue sky first appeared as a slit of color, steadily growing as the gray mantle above me receded ahead of the increasing wind from the favorable westerly quarter. Soon I was running fast under a rare blue cloudless sky. It seemed unnatural to be able to enjoy such a lovely day but the pleasant sky matched my mood as I cranked on all sail and set course for my waypoint off Cape Horn.

To round Cape Horn had never been an ambition in itself for me. All my life I had planned to circumnavigate the world and, depending on the route I chose, the Horn may or may not have been on the way. But as I found myself daily drawing nearer to what has for generations been described as the sailor's most outstanding landfall, the act or the achievement of rounding the southern tip of South America began to increase in significance for me. It seemed as if the object of leg three was to pass Cape Horn, almost as if that in itself completed the leg, with then only another week at sea to

Punta del Este. Passing the Horn became the focal point of the fleet radio conversations as it was the major turning point in the race. Once passed, it seemed that then we could relax and begin to head north to the warmer Atlantic waters and a break in Punta del Este.

Now that I had altered course and was steering north-east toward Cape Horn with such exhilarating weather I felt that I was really beginning to achieve something instead of perpetually heading east across the bottom of the planet. The Horn, Uruguay and my rendezvous with Cindy were getting closer by the minute.

▲ *Grey skies were normal in these Southern Ocean conditions*

My noon position put me 670 nautical miles from Cape Horn on a magnetic course of 45 degrees—about three days' sail away. The sky had been clear for about 4 hours, which was a rarity in these latitudes. I knew that I could not expect the good conditions to last for very much longer and there was already a telltale hint of cloud on the horizon. However, for a while longer I was able to enjoy a respite from the continual grey and damp that I had had for weeks. After remaining on deck enjoying the conditions until mid afternoon, I went down below to make an entry in my log and to check on my position and progress. Deciding to take a brief nap, I crawled into my bunk feeling that all was well with the world.

Obviously, how much sleep I could get a day related to the weather conditions, the amount of expected shipping and my proximity to land. Usually the rougher the weather the less sleep I got so in good-to-moderate conditions when the boat was in the groove, not needing much input from me, I would occasionally sneak some extra bunk time.

However, all was not to remain well with my world for much longer. I had been trying to sleep for about 20 minutes, really only enough time to thaw the bag out and start to enjoy the cosy warmth, when I felt *Newcastle Australia* power up and accelerate from the force of increased wind strength. It had been blowing 20 knots when I had gone down below but now it was blowing over 40 knots and the boat was hard-pressed, laying over, with the autopilot struggling to hold the heading. I scrambled out of bed, grabbed my jacket and raced to the helm at the back of the cockpit.

I was facing aft and grabbed the wheel to steer downwind to ease the pressure on the rig. At the same instant, as I turned to look forward, everything in my view went into slow motion. I saw the mast snap and the boat suddenly become upright as the 72 foot (22 m) mast and all of my sails toppled into the sea. I have no memory of what my first thoughts were but I realized that the spinnaker pole that I had been using, which was attached to the mast, was in the water. Nothing mattered but that I retrieve that pole. It would be a vital component in the jury rig that I would need to create if I was to sail myself out of here.

The spinnaker pole was fixed to the mast by a pivoting bell-shaped fitting, which I could not get to. Because the 25 foot (7.6 m) alloy pole was now full of water and was extremely heavy, I was unable to drag it aboard, so I lashed it in place to attend to later. I tied the free end to the bow but shortly after the bell-shaped fitting broke off the mast and the pole came free, so I was able to retrieve it.

I then set about getting tools to cut the rig away from the boat. The mast, which was now hanging vertically and attached by myriad rope and rods of stainless steel, was a real threat to the safety of the boat. With the wave motion lifting *Newcastle Australia* up and down, there was the threat of the jagged end of the broken extrusion puncturing the skin of the hull if the boat pounded down onto it.

The squall passed over and the wind settled down again to about 20 to 25 knots. The motion of the boat, without her mast and sails acting against the keel's pendulum motion, was incredible. Instead of a steady angle of heel, the boat whipped back and forth in rapid rolls every few seconds as

▲ *View of the foredeck of* Newcastle Australia *after her dismasting*

the swells passed under the hull. I scrambled around on deck armed with a knife, a hacksaw and a 3 foot (1 m) long pair of bolt cutters. I needed a variety of tools to cut away the rig. I was able to cut some of the rod rigging with bolt cutters, but the heavier shrouds had to be cut with the hacksaw. I was able to save the boom, which was still on board, by slashing the sail where it draped over the gunnel. Then the mast ripped off and started to sink. I cut ropes for about an hour until finally the mast was held on only by the forestay.

The boat's motion was frantic as I crawled along the narrow fore-deck to cut the stay. However, the bouncing and joggling of the boat made it too dangerous to try and saw through the half-inch (12 mm) thick metal turnbuckle. As the bow went over a wave, the waterlogged mast, sails and fittings resisted the bow's tendency to lift and it would load up suddenly with a jarring snap. This made it impossible for me to cut through this last turnbuckle. I had nothing to hold onto as the starboard rails were all ripped off the deck when the mast came down. The forestay's movement looked as if it would cut the front of the boat off. With each heart-rending crash, the bow would jerk up and slew down from the drag. Finally with a bang the heavy stainless steel turnbuckle stud broke and the mast and sails began their descent to the bottom of the 2500 fathom (5000 m) deep Pacific Ocean.

It was with relief I watched the potential danger go—but what a waste. My new mainsail and the beautiful Schaefer furling gear gone! My lovely boat was stripped with the deck looking like a field that had been ravaged by locusts.

By the time I had finally detached the rig, the wind was blowing at over 30 knots and seemed set to increase overnight. I took stock of what I had been able to salvage, which included my spinnaker poles, the boom and the lower panel of the mainsail, one set of running backstay blocks and what seemed to be miles of halyards. I had cut these and pulled them through the hollow mast extrusion before it sank. The ropes were now laying haphazardly about the deck so I set about securing everything for the night. I lashed the poles and boom snugly to the deck and began to coil the lengths of line.

Before it was dark I also managed to telephone race headquarters via AT&T on the single sideband radio to let them know of my dismasting. I had not lost my antenna, which was an 18 foot (5.5 m) whip aerial mounted on the transom. I was the most southern yacht in the fleet and felt very isolated. When I told Pete at headquarters of my predicament he took a quick check of my position and replied with 'too bad Alan, stay in touch'—click. He had terminated the call. I had not expected any sympathy but I thought a few moments of conversation might have been a welcome distraction.

The next call I made was to Cindy. She was typically bright and positive and we chatted for a while and talked about our options. We had none. Together we agreed that we had committed to finishing this race three years before and we would remain committed to our sponsors and to finishing it—even now. We thought that once I got to Uruguay I might be able to borrow a mast from a local yacht or buy a second hand one but that something would work out. We were determined to finish what we started.

After making the calls, I finished coiling the lines and hung them from the port lifelines. I fussed about making sure that everything was in order and arranged neatly. By now it was getting darker and a proper gale was blowing. *Newcastle Australia* was drifting downwind at 3 knots and I think my efforts to make the deck as neat as possible were a way of keeping my mind off the problems.

I knew how I would assemble the jury rig and I had everything with me that I would need to build a strong A-frame mast. I had read of this type of rig being used on other occasions and I assumed it would be similar to what Robin Davie was using further west. Later when I was speaking to

Niah I could hear some of the other skippers interjecting that 'I should take it easy' and that 'it wouldn't matter if I took a couple of days to get going again'. However, my reply was 'No way, I'm going to be sailing by lunchtime tomorrow'.

I certainly felt vulnerable way south on my own that night. I was concerned that if a severe storm hit me, when I had no way to keep the boat moving safely, I could be rolled as Isabelle had been in leg two. I had a pasta dish for dinner and then went to bed although I hardly slept as my mind was racing, thinking about my busy day on the morrow. I was praying for a solution and put my plans for the jury rig to God.

I was on deck at first light, which in the high southern latitudes was about 0400 hours. I was still in gale-force westerly winds and it was very bleak with low clouds, sleet and drizzle. I ate some leftover pasta and a Power bar for breakfast and began to assemble the jury rig. I felt an incredible peace and I was relaxed in my mind, with an amazing energy level. I was confident that I would be sailing by noon.

My plan was to lash the ends of the spinnaker poles together, forming an A shape. The two lower ends of the poles I would support at deck level by plugging them into the bell-shaped fittings used to attach the poles onto the front of the mast and lash them to the chain plates. The fittings had a universal joint, which I was able to use as a hinge to raise the new mast once I had assembled the components.

The first and one of the most difficult jobs was to turn the poles end for end. I needed to have the front end fittings on the poles aft in the cockpit so that I could join them as the new masthead, and the plug end fittings, which were for the mast base, needed to be forward as I set the rig up. In port or on a flat sea it would have been an easy task to lift the 25 foot (7.6 m) long poles and reverse their position. But to lift, balance and shift them on a violently rolling deck was extremely difficult and dangerous, made even more so by the lack of lifelines on the starboard side.

I lashed the bell-shaped ends of the poles to the chain plates on each side of the boat. Once that was done, I proceeded to lash the ends together, working in the aft end of the cockpit. Once the top end was tied firmly I attached blocks at the masthead for the mainsail and jib halyards, plus a spare block and halyard each. I also attached three Kevlar and Spectra forestays at the top and ran two of them at deck level through blocks aft to winches in the cockpit. The third forestay I tensioned up with a purchase of four to one at its base. I made provision for four backstays, and again I led the main ones to a winch in the cockpit. I hauled on all the halyards,

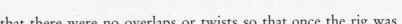

making sure that there were no overlaps or twists so that once the rig was up everything would be ready for use.

All through this the weather did not let up for a minute; in fact the wind strength had actually increased. The wet, I am unsure whether to call it rain or snow, continued unabated. Although the water temperature was down to about 35.6 degrees Fahrenheit (2 degrees Celsius), I wore only one layer of thermal clothing under my wet-weather gear. However, I had no time to feel the cold; indeed the constant activity on deck kept me warm enough to be comfortable. I was amazed at how well it all came together and because I was feeling so good and determined to be underway soon, I decided I would not take a break to rest or eat until I had set sail.

Once the A-frame was secured at top and bottom, the next step was to hoist it aloft using the forestays that I had led aft through blocks on deck. It was very difficult to lift this bi-pole arrangement off the deck as the hoisting halyard block was at the most forward point of the boat and such a long, shallow pulling angle gave little or no mechanical advantage. As I had to crank the winch handle to hoist the halyard I was limited to standing on the cockpit floor raising the bi-pole above my head using only one hand, grinding the winch with the other hand. Inch by inch it rose slowly to a point where I could no longer reach to push the frame and the halyard had no more purchase to lift the poles. The whole structure sat there almost in limbo. The pressure on the halyard was pulling the apex of the frame toward the front of the boat and compressing it against the base of the assembly, in effect, going nowhere.

In trying to determine what to do from here I suddenly remembered windsurfers doing water starts, utilizing the wind to lift both sail and rider out of the water after a capsize. I thought that maybe I could tie some sail fabric to the frame and use the wind to hoist the mast aloft but as it was gusting over 40 knots now I was not game to put sail cloth on the rig for lift in case I had trouble when it got up. I did not want any added dramas today.

I decided to compromise and use the wind conservatively. After setting two backstays at an approximate length so that the bi-pole could not fall forward once aloft, I adjusted the autopilot to steer dead downwind. Waiting for a gust, I squatted on the cabin top to get as much advantage as possible and heaved the rig as high as I could. As the boat rose to the top of a swell the wind increased. The gust was enough to give a bit of extra push and the mast stood vertically. It then toppled forward until the backstays were under tension. The rig was up!

I then had to take some slack out of the forestay and retension the backstays on the running backstay winches until the mast was plumb. I determined it should have some rake aft and eased the forestays slightly, resetting everything until I was satisfied it was a permanent solution. Once it was up, it all seemed so easy. I was ecstatic. After being without a mast above me for 20 hours the stumpy bi-pole appeared to tower over me.

I checked everything thoroughly and timidly set my storm jib on one forestay. Sheeting it on, *Newcastle Australia* gently heeled to the pressure and began to come alive as she picked up speed. It was a tremendous moment. It felt good to be alive! My wallowing boat was now sailing at an amazing 5 to 6 knots, back on course for the Horn. As the gale continued I was content to carry on with only the storm jib overnight, so as to test the rig out. I was glad to have taken the conservative route as my 35 to 40 knot wind built and by midnight was steady at more than 50 knots. Overnight, the stainless steel mount for the wind generator snapped.

Newcastle Australia surfed on some of the waves and we took off, touching 9 and 10 knots occasionally. The jury rig seemed to be holding up

▲ *View of the jury rig from aft showing how the spinnaker poles were attached to the chain plates*

▲ *View of the jury rig from forward*

extremely well, but I would regularly check on the ropes holding it all together. I was worried about chafe or that the lashings would work loose but everything settled in and gradually I became confident that the rig would see me through. I would look up so often to make sure that I still had a mast above me that the grossly inadequate bi-pole began to look 'normal'.

▶

*How the spinnaker pole
bell fitting was attached to
the chain plate*

The strong winds continued in the 40-plus range for the first two days of sailing with my jury rig and it was not until the Wednesday morning that the wind eased enough for me to dare to raise the storm trysail as a mainsail under the A-frame. The added sail area increased the available horse-power and I continued on at a steady daily average of between 125 and 150 miles. With the jury rig up my work load lessened considerably. With such a basic sail plan there were minimum adjustments to trim that I could make. The sails were either up or down, in or out. Provided that they

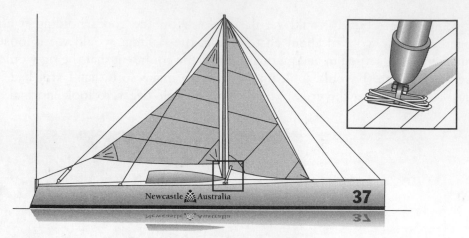

▲ *Diagram showing how the jury rig looked and how the pole fitting was lashed to the chain plate at deck level. With my 97 feet square (9 m square) storm jib and 190 feet square (18 m square) storm trysail I had a total sail area of 287 square feet (27 m square)*

were not flogging it did not seem to make much difference to boat speed as long as the wind stayed fresh from behind.

With my Standard-C fax out of action my only link was via the radio. I checked in with Niah each day, who was great, relaying any faxes that he may have received for me from home or race headquarters. I was heading directly for Punta del Este but meanwhile friends ashore were looking at the possibility of finding a mast that we could ship to the Falkland Islands. Of course the cost would be prohibitive but we had to explore every avenue to keep in the race.

We were aware that there was an Air Force jet leaving England on 6 March for the once a month cargo flight to the Falkland Islands. Robin Davie was making arrangements to ship his new mast on this plane. Josh Hall began to see what could be done for me. So with less than a week to organize everything, my passenger from leg one, Josh Hall, began working in the Charleston race headquarters with their offer to use the telephone and fax, and was able to locate a second-hand mast in England. The mast was old and available for an outrageous sum. In response to a reduced offer, the reply was 'You want to buy a mast? I have one to sell.' We were in quite a bind and did not have time for negotiations.

During the time that Josh was making preliminary investigations as to the logistics involved with the shipment, I was getting feedback about the people of Newcastle's reaction to my dismasting. In a radio interview the journalist said to me that they were receiving many calls from people who expressed everything from concern for me to offers of financial assistance. This was from ordinary citizens who had had no involvement to date with our campaign except from newspaper, television and radio reports of the race. The major theme that came from these contacts was that a large portion of the community was behind me and was determined to see me continue racing *Newcastle Australia* around the world.

Josh had now worked out some budget estimates to buy the mast, rig and second-hand sails, transport them from Grimsby in the north-east of England, then down to Southampton to be retrofitted with new spreaders to suit *Newcastle Australia*'s chainplate configuration, then shipped overland to Bryce Norton Air Force Base. This was a huge undertaking, with only five days for Josh to liaise and co-ordinate everything on the telephone and fax, with the time differences between the American east coast and England and Australia making smooth communications difficult.

I was totally blown away to hear by radio telephone that the Newcastle City Council had held a crisis meeting, voting to continue its involvement by extending a loan to the campaign to cover costs. The initial costing was for about $A30 000, which was to become $A45 000, a major component being the airfreight charges.

Once we knew that the money was available it was full steam ahead to the Falkland Islands and I altered course at best speed with an estimated time of arrival of 6 March. Before leaving Sydney I had anticipated arriving in Punta del Este before this date.

Josh and I made a list of all the necessary components that had to be ordered, as well as the rig modifications, which had to be designed and sent to Proctor Masts in Southampton. Henry Washburn and his team at Proctor Masts did a terrific job of making new spreaders, servicing the old rig and making up new halyards before packaging it up for shipping in record time. At the last minute they were told that the aircraft was to be loaded from the side door and not the rear door as previously indicated. This created more jobs as they then had to cut the mast in half and make joining sleeves that were pre-drilled and supplied with everything needed to fit the rig together in the Falkland Islands. Mark Reuther, the US agent for Pro-Furl, generously offered to ship some furling gear as my sponsors at Scheafer Marine were unable to ship anything in time due to some missed messages. Everything had to be thought out to the last detail, because we did not know what was available in the Falklands.

With the Falkland Islands now my target I could look forward to getting ashore within a week. After my dismasting Arnie Taylor on *Thursday's*

Child had changed course to the Falkland Islands because his mast was still a problem and he had decided it was not worth the risk to continue on, possibly ending up like Robin and me. It looked as though there would be a crowd in Port Stanley while we were there.

I continued on, drawing nearer to Cape Horn each day, although it was a less exciting prospect rounding it in a crippled yacht. The other skippers reported fantastic roundings surfing past the landmark in gale-force winds. I was a little depressed knowing that now there was no way that I could come third overall for Class II. The weather remained bleak and uninspiring with steady gale-force winds. But the reality was that I was making great progress with the small rig and, providing the wind did not come from the east, I could count on a consistent daily average into Port Stanley.

The winds remained favorable, strong from the west and south-west, and I steadily gained on the infamous Horn.

1 MARCH
My log reads:

If weather holds will be around corner [the Horn] day after tomorrow, which will be good—I am ready to get out of the Southern Ocean, that's for sure. Arnie and Niah have been pretty encouraging, they are almost in the Atlantic and cheered up considerably.

The next day I received word that Harry Mitchell's EPIRB had been activated. The deep low pressure cell that I had been watching to the west had developed into a severe storm with hurricane-force winds at over 70 knots. It had overtaken Harry's position and must have caused some real damage for tough old Harry to set off a distress alarm. We all held hopes for him because Minoru was behind him and conceivably would be able to pick him up. But Minoru was having troubles of his own and on the same day lost all electrical power. He never received word of Harry's plight and indeed we thought he too had been overwhelmed. There were no reports from him for another week, when a ship searching for Harry saw him and reported him battling on with no power.

Two merchant vessels searched a huge area, covering thousands of square miles in gale-force conditions until they were forced to abandon the search and continue on their own course due to low fuel and dangerous seas. There was no word received from Harry or any sign of his vessel, *Henry*

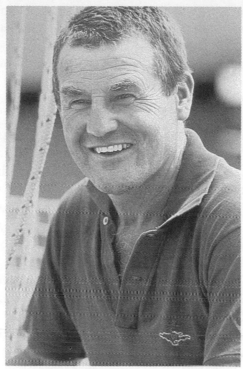

▲ *Harry Mitchell*   BILLY BLACK/BOC

Hornblower. It was to be several weeks before the official pronouncement was made—that he was lost at sea. Harry had died in the pursuit of a childhood dream to sail past Cape Horn. This was his third attempt in a small yacht with limited resources and even though he was not able to physically achieve the dream, Harry's dogged determination and frank sense of humor was an inspiration to each of us that were out there with him in the pursuit of our own dreams.

That same day five skippers crossed the finish line into Punta del Este over a 5-hour period, making up one of the tightest finishes. Steve Pettingill followed by Jean Luc Van den Heede, then Giovanni Soldini, David Adams and JJ Provoyeur. It was incredible that after more than thirty-one days at sea, each sailing different boats and different courses, this highly competitive group could finish so close. Christophe on *Sceta Calberson* had already arrived two and a half days earlier to consolidate his overall lead, having won both southern legs.

On the evening of Thursday 2 March I passed south of the Diego Ramirez Group and could see the light on Isla Gonzalo from about 17 miles. There was a ship to the west of the island and I spoke to them on VHF radio. Their response was in English but wiped out by static—a little disappointing. It was a brilliant night, about my third night for the leg where I could see stars overhead. The Horn was 60 miles away and I was on course at 6.3 knots.

The swell pattern had changed suddenly as Isla Gonzalo came into view and I crossed onto the continental shelf. One of the reasons for the Horn's notoriety is the fact that the water depth suddenly drops from several thousand fathoms to between 50 and 100 fathoms. My track on the chart put me in an area where over a distance of 5 to 6 miles the ocean depth went from 2000 to 70 fathoms. The shallower water created a short, sharp chop, which on a rough day must be horrendous. However, my steady south-west breeze at 25 knots did not cause the 13 to 16 feet (4 to 5 m) seas to be dangerous—but the sharp triangular peaks spoke of their potential.

Arnie on *Thursday's Child* was approaching the Falkland Islands and Niah had passed the Horn the day before. He was in light winds and heading up through the Straits of Le Maire, a 15-mile wide strait separating the south-eastern tip of Argentina and Isla de los Estados. Once through he would be in the South Atlantic Ocean and he sounded cheerful on the radio. I was next in line.

At 0800 hours local time on the third day of the third month on my thirty-third day at sea, my log records:

> Passed the infamous Cape Horn, 1300 zulu, blue sky and fresh south-west wind ... good to know God's grace keeps me alright.

While passing the Horn I was reflective, sitting on the cabin top wondering if I should be excited or if this was merely another headland. I had closed to within 4 miles and was enjoying the view of Isla Hornos and the steep profile that outlined the famous Cape. I suddenly felt a rush of excitement—the thought of all the miles I had sailed to be here, of the opportunities and people that had allowed me to come. I dashed below to grab my camera. This was an achievement, though not mine alone.

Not long after I had doubled the Cape a series of squalls with sleet and gusts of 40 knots hit me for an hour or so, and I scooted off east towards the Falkland Islands and the South Atlantic Ocean. However, once past the

▲ *The infamous Cape Horn—not just another headland!*

Cape the seas began to flatten out as the breeze slacked off in the lee of the land. I now had 400 miles to go to the Falkland Islands, hopefully only three more days. For several hours I could see the land receding in view and I wondered if I would be back this way again.

Two more days of good progress followed with winds from the west and very rough, steep seas. My log reads 'copping a hiding ... choppy'. The Sunday brought a pleasant change, although light winds, and I recorded my slowest day of jury-rigged sailing, covering only 100.8 miles in 24 hours. By 0400 hours on Monday 6 March I was in sight of Beauchene Island, a long, low, flat rock, the southernmost island in the Falkland group. I had almost 90 miles left to travel to Cape Pembroke and the entrance to Stanley Harbour. Once clear of Beauchene Island I had to alter course to work up closer to the main island group. It was imperative that I stay close under the lee of the land as I could not risk being blown downwind of the islands. *Newcastle Australia* would not sail to windward with such a clumsy sail plan.

It was an exciting, although unwanted, landfall and all that day I sailed in sight of the low islands. I was in radio contact with Martin Cox, a 'Kiwi' living on the islands who managed a local fishing consortium. He passed on some local knowledge and relayed updates to Ian Doherty and Robin

Goodwin from the Falkland Island Company (FIC), who had offered to be on standby to tow me in once I had made it under my own steam to the harbor mouth.

Arnie Taylor of *Thursday's Child* had arrived a couple of days previously. I spoke to him on the radio and he raved about the local hospitality and the night-life. Two of his shore crew, Merf Owen and Kate Ford, had flown in to work on his yacht.

For a while it looked as though I would arrive before dark but the wind remained light and fickle as I drifted along at 3 knots in unexpected sunshine. I really had to pay attention and watch my course because there was a strong current running along the coast that tended to set me to seaward or east of the island. With a forecasted northerly wind, I was apprehensive about getting too far offshore and struggling to beat back. However, I made reasonable progress into the night and I passed on a new estimated time of arrival of around 0300 hours at Cape Pembroke.

The northerly began to build, causing me to pinch my inefficient rig up as high as possible to the wind—I was only just able to keep my course creeping past the rocky shore. I had to dodge the partly submerged and unlit Wolf and then Seal Rocks. With the wind now gusting at 25 to 30 knots flying spray was continually shooting over me at the helm—the night was as black as soot and very cold.

With only a couple of miles to go, Ian Doherty called me on VHF radio to say that they were heading out to meet me for the tow into Stanley Harbour. I was cheered by the news that Arnie, Merf and Kate were aboard to welcome me in. Once I was past Cape Pembroke I eagerly looked for the lights of the pilot boat *Speedwell*. We called each other on the VHF radio and they were frustrated that I was not visible on radar. I could see the bright lights of the pilot boat but they, forgetting my mast was only a stump, were expecting to see my masthead navigation lights. Not until I shone a bright spotlight did they see me and alter course to *Newcastle Australia*'s position.

It was not until *Speedwell* was abeam of *Newcastle Australia* that I realized how rough the conditions were. After weeks of seeing nothing but Southern Ocean rollers my perspective must have been off. I thought the conditions were reasonable, although choppy, causing me to be wet and cold all night. But when I saw the powerful looking 40 foot (12.2 m) pilot boat being buffeted by waves and disappearing into the swells, the comparison was amazing. Their boat looked far too small to be out on such a night. I felt admiration for these people who had come to lend a hand and welcome me in.

I crawled forward on *Newcastle Australia*'s twisting, bucking foredeck to lower the sails and prepare to take a line aboard for the tow. No word could be heard above the din of the roaring engines and the pelting spray. Once the tow line was connected we headed into the harbor at 8 knots, directly into the wind and chop. Lashed with icy spray from *Speedwell*'s wake, I was never so cold and wet as I steered, relieved to have finally arrived.

CHAPTER TEN

Intermission in the Falklands

I ARRIVED in the Falkland Islands on Tuesday 6 March, almost thirty-seven days since I had departed Sydney. That warm summer day seemed like another era. Once tied up behind *Thursday's Child* at the FIC floating barge, Arnie and his shore crew, Merf and Kate, took me ashore and we headed off to the Warah guesthouse where they had booked a room for me.

My first choice was whether to eat breakfast first or have a shower. I did not look back as I threw my bag in a room and headed off to soak under the luxuriant flow of steaming, hot, fresh water. My body tingled, revitalized after five weeks clad in thermal clothing and heavy wet-weather clothing. I then enjoyed a hearty English breakfast of eggs, sausages and bacon, with toast and jam and cups of tea, followed by a couple of hours of sleep in a warm, dry, motionless bed.

Arnie and his team were busy getting things sorted out on *Thursday's Child* and had hauled the mast out of the boat the day before. They had hired an old four-wheel drive and offered to cart me around with them.

I had originally hoped to have a quick stopover, estimating four days as enough time to fit the mast. However, I received word that the mast would not arrive until the Thursday as the flight from England had been delayed. I was not too hassled by this, really just grateful that it was coming at all. I made a list of things that I could do by myself, such as strip the jury rig and sort the boat out in readiness for the rest of the leg—on up to Uruguay.

▲ Newcastle Australia *tied to the floating dock in Stanley Harbour.* Thursday's Child *is behind and its mast is laying on the dock* KATE FORD

The facility that we had tied to in Stanley Harbour was an old steel barge, leftover from the military occupation during the Falkland's War in the early 1980s. It was a huge floating structure equipped with warehouses and machine shops, even barrack-style accommodation and the fisheries department office. It was used to repair fishing vessels that worked year round in the rugged Southern Ocean waters.

Arnie had his mast laying along the length of 'our' section and as well as his shore crew he had the local machinists and welders busy at work on a new mast base. We were both lucky to have Carl's and Andres' skill and enthusiasm at our disposal. They worked for FIC and were both keen yachtsmen, happy to work on some sailboats for a change. Carl was an Australian and he and his wife had sailed to the Falkland Islands fifteen years before via Cape Horn and had decided to make the Falklands their home. They were in the process of completing a new steel cruising yacht for some planned voyages to the Antarctic.

Another amazing occurrence happened at this time that no one could have planned or foreseen. About eighteen months before we had solicited

▲ *Taking down my jury rig in the calm of Stanley Harbour*

the support of an Australian company, Howard Smith Limited. They are a huge corporation with links to Newcastle but with marine and shipping interests worldwide. Their initial decision to join our support group with a medium-level sponsorship was most welcome. However, while I was sailing under jury rig the Australian chief executive officer, David Webb, whom I had never met, read of my dilemma and that I was headed for the Falklands. Realizing that Howard Smith had an ocean-going salvage tug based in the South Atlantic Ocean, he immediately took the initiative to inform us that their tug, *The Indomitable*, was stationed in the Falklands and that the captain and crew would render whatever assistance they could.

This was terrific news. I had a telephone number for the tug and was surprized to hear that the day before I arrived they had moved the ship to Mare Harbour further south on the island. They were involved with some military ship movements. However, my contact, Tim Richardson, and the captain were most helpful and arranged for the ship's agent to visit me to see what could be done. When the agent, a retired merchant sea captain, arrived at the boat he was full of enthusiasm for my voyage and passed on well-wishes from the crew of *The Indomitable*. He shoved a fistful of British money at me and instructed me to book anything, such as accommodation, meals and telephone calls, to *The Indomitable*'s account. This was an incredible convenience and saved the delays and hassles associated with trying to find and have money wired from Australia. That simple offer to chip in and help from Howard Smith's management was a major factor in keeping us going. I had arrived with zero dollars (where do you shop in the Southern Ocean?) and was quite embarrassed and worried about this, not wanting to run the risk of appearing to assume on the local people's hospitality or generosity. With that pressure taken off me I was able to concentrate on the matters at hand.

Down on the dock work was progressing on *Thursday's Child*'s mast, while I set about dismantling my jury rig. It almost seemed a pity to have to take it down. Taking the bi-pole down in a safe harbor was a much quicker operation than it had been to put it in place originally. I soon had it all on deck and began to sort the salvageable from the unsalvageable. My two spinnaker poles I would keep and, of course, much of the rope I could use again on board, although many of the lengths had been cut up and would be too short to use as halyards. I gave some to an appreciative Andres for his cruising boat because good modern synthetic lines suitable for small boats were hard to come by in the Falklands.

► *Arnie Taylor, Merf Owen and Kate Ford working on* Thursday's Child

The following day was quite relaxing although frustrating with not a lot to do. I could only wait for the mast to arrive. Of course there were routine chores for me to do but the boat was in good shape except for the rig. Also, after some rest, the novelty of being ashore had worn off and I began to fret about the delay and the fact that the 'racing' clock was continuing to tick over.

Kate Ford had brought with her a new IBM Thinkpad computer to replace mine that had drowned earlier in the leg. It was set up with the software that the fleet were using for weather and satellite communications. I installed it and checked that I was back on line. It was good to know I would have the weather and fax capabilities for the sprint up to Punta del Este.

Thursday morning arrived and it felt like Christmas. The mast was due in mid morning and it had been arranged that Robin Goodwin from FIC would drive me the 20 miles out to the military air base in a twelve ton tip truck to collect mine and *Cornwall*'s gear. I climbed up into the truck feeling very excited and settled in for the drive to the base. Robin had been born and raised in the Islands and proudly began to bring me up to date with some Island history, pointing out things of interest along the way. It only took about 5 minutes to clear the town limits and we travelled over country devoid of trees, the only cover being a coarse yellow grass. We could see the sea and coastline for most of the hour-long trip and we passed fenced-off areas in the middle of nowhere. Signs were posted with cautionary notices—Danger: uncleared minefield—remnants of the war between Britain and Argentina that was fought during April and May 1982.

We arrived at the miliary base and, after meeting the Lieutenant Colonel in charge of the base, also a keen yachtsman, we were cleared to pick up the shipment. Once in the warehouse it was obvious to whom the two long packages belonged. After checking off the manifest we noticed that some of my bags of sails and coils of line were missing. After a little panic I located the errant pieces in another warehouse a few minutes later, they having been sent there by mistake.

We began the return trip with me feeling incredibly blessed. I was thrilled, knowing how much had been achieved in the last few days and that soon I would be back at sea. Once back at the dock, we unloaded and sorted *Cornwall*'s gear from mine and cleared space in the warehouse to set up my new rig. Anthony Boalch, Robin Davie's rigger from England, was flying in the next day. Josh Hall had arranged for us to share some of his expenses by paying half his airfare and an hourly rate for the time that he worked on my rig. This worked out well and, by the time Anthony Boalch arrived on the Friday evening, I had unpacked everything ready for him to assemble according to the instructions that Proctor Masts had given him before leaving England.

Once Anthony Boalch arrived things began to happen much faster. He had the tools and skill to set things up with a minimum of fuss. He was dismayed to see the 10 foot (3 m) section that remained from my original mast and pointed out some apparently basic flaws in the design and way it had been made, exclaiming that it was amazing it had not fallen down sooner.

The new mast was slightly shorter than my original mast but it went together remarkably well, the joining pieces fitting perfectly, and the new spreaders looking strong and reassuring. It looked as though I could be ready to leave by Tuesday. After two days in the workshop we were ready to step the mast on the Monday. *Thursday's Child*'s mast was back up and I was glad the crane operator had some practice.

▶ *The new mast being stepped on* Newcastle Australia

My mast went up with a few triumphant cheers but once up there were many small adjustments to be made before we could tune it and set it up finally. We had to make new backstays out of leftover kevlar line and run new halyards and set the standing rigging tight. My original boom had to be fitted and a new gooseneck location had to be determined. Life rails had to be welded in the shed and the roller furling gear had to be set up and the sails bent on. We spent hours up the mast ensuring the spreaders were covered with cloth and tape to resist chafe on the sails. On the Tuesday, my last day, we had Kate helping with the running rigging as *Thursday's Child* was all but finished.

Arnie was scheduled to leave about noon and once he and Merf had finished, Ian and Robin on *Speedwell* towed him out of the inner harbor. I was determined to beat Arnie to Punta del Este. We raced all afternoon in an effort to finish my boat so that I could leave before nightfall. We had a problem with the position of the boom gooseneck, as the boom dragged on deck with the sail hoisted, and we had to resite it. It was 1730 hours when, after some fiddling, Anthony Boalch finally did the last bolt up. As he put his tools ashore we passed *Speedwell* a line, casting off from the rusted steel dock that had been my berth for the week. I raised the new mainsail for the first time as we motored across Stanley Harbour.

Merf and Kate came along for the tow and after a few minutes they stepped over onto *Speedwell* wishing me a fast passage. I threw them the tow line, waved and shouted my thanks to everyone, unfurled my new (ancient) spectra genoa, and headed off in pursuit of *Thursday's Child*.

CHAPTER ELEVEN

Down but not out

It WAS a clear, crisp evening as I sailed away from Port Stanley. Once I had cast off from *Speedwell* I had just enough daylight to sail safely clear of the larger bay that protected the inner harbor at Stanley. I was apprehensive about my replacement mast as it was untried and seemed huge after sailing for a thousand miles with only the stumpy jury rig above the deck.

I had been in the Falkland Islands for seven days and was relieved beyond belief to be at sea again. For the past couple of days a severe gale had been blowing with 50 knot winds from the north. I had been concerned at the thought of leaving for Punta del Este in such conditions but the day of my and Arnie Taylor's departure turned out to be mild with light winds. However, the wind was expected to build in the night from the north-north-west. I was glad to have an easy 15 knot wind to head out on, even if it meant sailing close-hauled. The moon was almost full and for the first part of the night my course was straight up the silver track made by its reflection on the smooth Atlantic swells. I stood on deck considering my good fortune at being here. My first log entry recorded my elation.

6 March
My log reads:

What an incredible thing has happened. I am almost in shock!! God is good. Humble thanks to all the people who have helped.

The wind began to change slightly as I cleared land, allowing me to sail closer to my course of 7 degrees true. Punta del Este was 1000 miles away at latitude 35 degrees south. This trip should be easy. With every mile I would be travelling north and the temperature would be getting warmer. I was still at 51 degrees south but it seemed as though the worst was over with the Horn and the great Southern Ocean behind me. If conditions were right, I could sail the distance in four to six days. I would arrive in Punta del Este about two weeks before the 1 April restart—plenty of time to prepare for the final leg to Charleston and maybe even a few quiet days with Cindy.

I had a lot to look forward to. The prospect of a quick passage up to Uruguay was made even more interesting by knowing that I would be able to race *Thursday's Child*. Arnie and I had arranged to update one another by checking in each morning and evening on single sideband radio.

The noise that the boat was making as she moved along at a steady 8 knots seemed extremely loud and actually intimidating with the water gurgling and swooshing as it flowed along the hull. I realized that I was not used to this noise because, while I sailed with a jury rig, *Newcastle Australia* had been whisper quiet. Even though I had made a consistent daily average with such minute sail area, the boat had sailed dead flat with no heel, hardly even making a wake and gently slipping along over the water. It was not normally until at a speed of about 9 knots with the boat about to plane before you could hear much noise of the water through the foam-cored hull. It had always seemed a healthy sound, knowing that she was sailing at good speed, but now mixed with the pop, thump and slap noises of the partly filled water ballast tanks it seemed strange to hear the boat moving so swiftly. My senses would soon adjust, however, as I settled back after my week-long sojourn on land.

The next morning it began to rain heavily and the wind eased off until I was only making about 1 to 2 knots of speed through the water. I had company during this calm spell when an albatross landed on the water by the boat's stern and then proceeded to leapfrog me. It would fly about a boat length ahead of *Newcastle Australia*, alight on the water, wait until I had drifted past and was at its original position by my stern and then fly past me again, landing on the water again. It repeated this casual process for most of the day.

The rain heralded a change and in the evening the wind returned from the westerly quarter. I began to sail on course, averaging about 8 knots. I was making good boat speed but *Newcastle Australia*'s performance was definitely off pace compared with the original rig and sail plan. My new mast had a fractional rig with the forestay attaching at three-quarters of the height of the mast. Thus, my sail area was limited to a short-hoist genoa and an ill-fitting mainsail with a reef permanently tied to keep the boom off the deck. My spinnakers were available but I had yet to test them and was looking forward to suitable conditions. I was actually quite nervous with a little bit of mast-drop paranoia creeping in.

My daily schedules with Arnie were usually encouraging, with both of us looking forward to the journey's end. The distance between us remained, with Arnie about 60 miles ahead of me. However, I had a few days to work on that.

After 48 hours I had made over 300 miles on my course, all good miles that I did not have to repeat. Miles achieved were like money in the bank, although I usually counted backwards, with the reduction in the distance to go being what yielded the highest returns.

That night I turned the folded chart over to reveal Punta del Este—my Mecca—that elusive landfall. No longer was I looking at the bottom of our world. Goodbye Cape Horn, goodbye Falkland Islands. So far this leg had taken me forty-seven days and I was already more than twelve days passed my anticipated arrival date. But everything was looking good and I could cope with a few more days at sea. The weather looked promising for a fast ride, with a full moon, and this short leg would be good preparation, allowing me to become familiar with the replacement rig and sails so that I could sail leg four with a vengeance.

At 0300 hours on Friday morning, 17 March, I was awakened by my off-course alarm on my autopilot—a rare occurrence as my Coursemaster autopilots performed so well. I went on deck and the moon was full, casting a brilliant light over the sea, which was running at about 13 feet (4 m). The boat was almost hove-to with the jib aback and stopped. I was not unduly concerned as the symptoms seemed similar to the occasion several weeks before when *Newcastle Australia* had slid up onto a huge floating kelp bed, about as big as a housing block of land, losing all way. I lost about one and a half hours by the time I extricated myself out of the tangle.

Looking over the side of the boat I could not see any kelp, if that was what it was. Maybe I had just tangled with some stray lengths of thick weed and the drag had caused the boat to stop in the choppy swell. I eased the mainsheet and grabbed the wheel to try and steer *Newcastle Australia* off the wind and get moving again. After several and various attempts, nothing happened.

Perhaps there was something wrong with the steering wires that connected the helm to the rudder quadrant. I raced below and up the stoopway that led under the deck to the aft compartment. Opening the hatch in the watertight bulkhead that separated the aft part of the boat, I shone a torch in to inspect the steering system but nothing was obviously wrong. The cables appeared fine and had the correct amount of tension. What could it be?

I was perplexed, struggling to determine what the problem could be. I went on deck again and, after several frustrating attempts to maneuver the boat, I was able to backwind the sails, forcing the boat over onto the other tack, only to have her instantly round up into the wind again, with the boom crashing over. Still no control. I was certain that something was drastically wrong but was unable to admit to myself that I had a problem with my rudder.

I hung over the side of the boat and peered into the water. Normally I could see the keel and rudder through the water. Tonight with the bright moonlight the visibility was exceptional and I could see the keel but no rudder. I told myself that it must be in the shadow of the hull.

My heart started to pound. I could not have lost the rudder—we had built it so strongly. I tore back into the aft compartment and rechecked the cables, which were fine. I was devastated. As the reality sank in, the accumulated stress and anxiety that I had been holding back, from weeks of delays and frustrations, the gales down south and then the dismasting, seemed to weigh heavily on my heart. However, I did not have the energy to feel angry. Instead, I felt crushed and cried with frustration. I wrote in my log as if to confirm the truth.

> **17 March**
> My log reads:
>
> 0530 ... Lost steering 2 hours!! ago.

Not long after I had admitted this I had to face another dilemma. I sensed that *Newcastle Australia* seemed heavy and I could hear a strange sound mixed with the many water noises that are part of everyday life on board. For the third time that morning I headed aft through the stoopway to the aft compartment and the noise became much louder. I could see into the stern watertight compartment through the clear Lexan bulkhead hatch and, to my horror, saw the aft compartment flooded with tons of sea water. As the boat rolled a 2 foot (0.6 m) high wave roared from side to side— inside my boat!

I poked my head through the hatch when the wave was on the side away from the opening and peered in. I could see a vertical crack and a solid stream of water coming from the base of the fiberglass tube where the rudder shaft passed through the hull. We must have hit something in the water, which had broken the rudder off. The rudder had been connected to the boat by a 4 inch (100 mm) diameter stainless steel tube, which had an inch (25 mm) wall thickness at the bearing where it came through the hull. The impact must have levered the bearing surface, cracking the tube. This day was not shaping up to be very happy.

Earlier I had sent a message to Arnie on the Standard-C telling him of my situation. He was standing by on single sideband radio waiting to hear from me. I radioed to him that the rear third of *Newcastle Australia* was flooding. Visions of *Gartmore Investment Managers* and Josh bailing flashed through my mind. I needed time to assess the damage and, with Arnie only 60 miles away, it was reassuring to be able to tell someone what was going on. Arnie offered to stand by on the radio and slowed *Thursday's Child* down in case I needed a hand.

Obviously, my first priority was to stem the flow of water—but how could I work inside a rolling barrel full of water? I hate getting wet and it was cold. I could not just blithely hop in as I knew it may take some time to effect the repairs and the cold numbing water would quickly zap my energy.

I amazed myself by quickly coming up with a plan to fix the leak. By joining a number of hose clamps (jubilee clips), I made two stainless steel straps long enough to wrap around the 8 inch (200 mm) diameter fiberglass tube where the rudder shaft passed through. It seemed logical that the gap would close back up when the clamps were adjusted tightly around the circumference of the tube. It would probably not be watertight but surely it would reduce the flow of water.

Typically, two heads are better than one. I was planning to grin and bear it, jumping into the swirling, cold, washing tub aft, when I decided to tell Arnie of my plan. He brilliantly suggested that I don my survival suit. The BOC rules demanded that we each carry on board an insulated neoprene suit designed to reduce the effects of exposure in survival situations, such as life raft or abandon ship scenarios. I had stowed mine before the race start and had hardly given it another thought, except when it was in the way when I looked for something stored nearby. Now the bright red-orange rubber suit seemed as valuable as gold to me.

Clad in my now extremely valuable one-piece suit of armor, I was totally encapsulated, including my gloved fingers and toes. Only my face remained exposed. I pumped the bilge pumps for several minutes to reduce the amount of water in the compartment before climbing in with my metal straps, bits of string and screwdriver. I was in the fray for only a few minutes, rolling from side to side with the torrents of water still in the compartment. I was grateful and relieved to see the gap close up beautifully as I tightened the clamps until there was only a small trickle of water weeping from the crack. Thank God for that—to be dealt with so quickly.

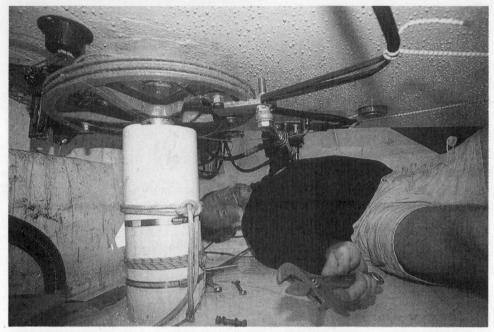

▲ *Christian Brit, shore crew from* Sceta Calberson, *helping to fix my rudder shaft in Punta del Este. You can see the hose clamps that I used to tighten the tube to stop the water rushing in*   BILLY BLACK

I must have been beaming as I reported to Arnie my success. But now I had to determine a method of steering *Newcastle Australia*. I was 600 miles south of Punta del Este and 400 miles east of Cabo Dos Bahías in Argentina. The logical and most expedient route was to head directly for Punta del Este. Arnie had lost his rudder on leg two and had amazingly sailed over 2000 miles with an emergency rudder that later fell off. Then, by dragging buckets and ropes, he steered *Thursday's Child* into Hobart for repairs. He told me about his experience using drogues. Not wanting to shun his advice, I tried it but with no success.

My state of mind at this stage was very low but the effort in the morning to fix the leak in the aft compartment had been a blessing in disguise. The need for immediate action had caused me to think and deal with a basic repair. This had given me a much-needed sense of achievement and probably helped me to pull out of the potential despair that I felt at the loss of the rudder. Even so, I was in the process of taking on my biggest challenge.

0930 17 MARCH
My log reads:

Not sure what to do to steer—maybe a pole and life jacket?

After my lack of success with the drogue method I went back to my original idea and set about using my small spinnaker pole as a steering oar. Once again, the well-designed Ronstan spinnaker pole bell fittings that had served me so well as mast tabernacles for the jury rig turned out to be one of the most versatile fittings on board. I lashed one of the bell-shaped universal joints onto the mounting pole for the wind generator at the very back of the cockpit. I then attached lines to the very end of the pole and ran these through blocks on the corners of the transom stern. These lines were then led to the running backstay winches in the cockpit.

Before pushing the 15 feet (4.5 m) pole off the back of the boat and connecting it to the pivoting joint, I took my top companionway washboard, a small panel used to close off the companionway in rough weather, and drilled a series of holes along this, lashing it onto the end of the pole to form a small paddle. I then attached an empty, plastic 5 gallon (20 L) fuel can to the pole to act as a float and to add some positive surface area to assist the 'oar' to control the boat. When the assembled steering oar was extended off the back of the boat, the control lines from each quarter helped secure and locate the oar, creating a rudimentary rudder or paddle.

1900 17 MARCH
My log reads:

I tried my pole idea—I think it works. We are steering 000 to 030 degrees at 3 to 4 knots. God willing, wind will stay in west for couple of days. Have a tiny bit of jib and main up. Cindy gets in tonight.

The jury rudder in action

The boat was now moving and basically in the right direction but it was a constant struggle for me to remain positive. On the Saturday I sailed all through the night but at a severely reduced speed. At around 1000 hours the wind built up from the south-west at about 25 to 35 knots. The seas became very rough, making it difficult to maintain a straight course. It was heartbreaking weaving a crooked course at 6 to 8 knots, on the edge of control and knowing that in similar conditions a healthy *Newcastle Australia* would be occasionally surfing at over 15 knots and easily averaging 10 to 11 knots with perfect control.

In the afternoon the boat slewed off a lumpy little wave and crash gybed. It took more than 90 minutes to get the boat to gybe safely back across— the steep, sharp waves were making control almost impossible. I felt cursed

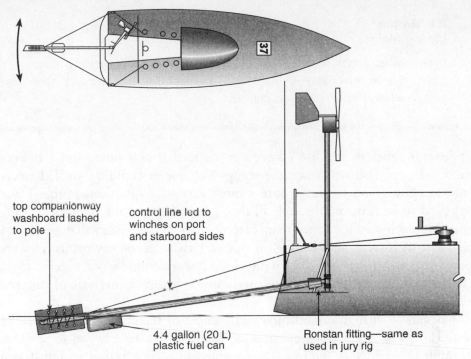

top companionway
washboard lashed
to pole

control line led to
winches on port
and starboard sides

4.4 gallon (20 L)
plastic fuel can

Ronstan fitting—same as
used in jury rig

▲ *Diagram showing the jury rudder steering arrangement*

by a favorable wind. The jury rudder was not an efficient steering device. To call it a rudder is probably a misnomer as it was actually more of a tracking aid, helping to keep the boat reasonably on course. The steering or control part mainly resulted from the sail trim. I constantly had to be watching and correcting sail balance to suit the changeable weather and swell patterns.

Physically I felt very weak and found I did not have much reserve left—the hours on deck keeping the boat tracking knocked me around. In my log I listed feelings of failure, rejection, embarrassment and apology.

Cindy arrived safely in Punta del Este on the Saturday but instead of making me feel closer to her and excited about our forthcoming reunion I had an increased feeling of isolation and frustration at my slow progress. Even telephone communication was futile, as I tended to sound like a whinger when I described the pressure. Cindy was always positive and I also spoke to David Adams and Mark Schrader, who both offered ideas and encouraged me to push on. To know that I was racing and losing ground was exhausting—I felt as though I was failing a big test.

21 MARCH
My log reads:

I panic when I look at the chart and realize that we have only made 220 miles in four days—400 to go. This is killing me. It never goes away—always slow, never on course.

Several times in my life I have experienced tough times and I believe that God used them to teach me things—character-building stuff. I never came to blame God for my troubles but I earnestly questioned what I was supposed to be learning through all this. I have been in the habit of reading the Bible each day for more than fifteen years and realized that perhaps I had been so focused for so long on this race that maybe my priorities were out of line in my relationship with God. I was reminded of a verse from Isaiah where the writer exclaimed 'surely it was for my benefit that I suffered such anguish'.

I began to change my attitude and instead of feeling sorry for myself I started to look at the circumstances of where I was at. I began to see that although this trip was the focus of so much publicity and attention it also was a personal voyage, where I would be pushed to limits I had never known. Hopefully, I would grow through this. I found renewed strength, both physically and mentally, as I began to spend more time reading the Bible, deciding to trust that God would enable me to break through.

After the south-westerly gale, the wind backed and came from the north, switching between the north-east and north-west. My jury rudder forced me to have reduced sail area, so once again on this voyage I had an inefficient rig and had great difficulty working to windward. For the 24 hours between Tuesday 21 March and Wednesday 22 March, I sailed over 100 miles but made only 15 miles over the ground toward my destination.

Thus, my goals had to be amended yet again. Instead of racing for a place, or even mixing it with *Thursday's Child* for the quick sprint to Punta del Este, I began to look over my shoulder as Robin Davie on *Cornwall* had now left the Falkland Islands with a new rig and at this rate would overtake me. I became determined to make it to Punta del Este by 26 March, which was Cindy's twenty-ninth birthday. This became my overruling mission in life—surely I could sail 400 miles in four days.

During the night I was enveloped in a sea fog, which was unreal and unexpected. The sea was flat and we trickled along. I woke to the sound of an Asian voice shouting 'mayday ... mayday' over the VHF radio. VHF is a limited-range radio, designed for line of sight communications, both ship to ship and ship to shore. Generally, my set was good for distances of 20 to 40 miles. The mayday distress signal was booming in so that whoever it was had to be very close.

I tried to contact the person over the radio but to no avail. Shortly after I heard another booming voice over the radio. It was a salvage tug, the *Warrior*, based out of Montevideo, Uruguay. They were en route to the vessel, which turned out to be a 700 ton Chinese fishing boat that was without power and had been drifting for a couple of days. I was able to listen in as they finally made contact and were secured for the 350 mile tow.

I spoke to the captain of the tug several times. They could only travel slowly under tow and we were making a similar speed. We crossed paths in sight of each other once or twice as my course was more erratic than their beeline to Montevideo.

The next day I only covered 67 miles. Then, incredibly, on Thursday I travelled 139.5 miles toward my goal, almost close-hauled in a 20 to 25 knot north-westerly. I felt like I had won a jackpot prize. By my reckoning that run was worth over three days to me. How our expectations change.

I had 186 miles to go to Punta del Este. On the next day's run, Friday, I averaged 4 knots on track. This was good. At sunset I saw a whale, and the wind went to another location. That night the weather was atrocious. A low overcast sky built and the clouds appeared squally and unstable. It was a very frustrating night as I continually had to alter course because of fickle, alternating breezes. My log the following morning summed it up.

25 MARCH
My log reads:

Last night was amazing, up nearly all night. Wind went, north-east, north-north-east, east, then west, south-west to north-west, then gale, then eased and went north, then west-south-west. She wouldn't run off with main up so dumped that and then was too slow with only jib. Tack then gybe all over. Finally gave up and went to bed at 0530—left boat to tend herself. Woke up to find wind eased and gone north-west. Good course and speed. I need 025 true for 114 miles. I set main, shook reefs and instantly reefed again!! It is a nice day.

By noon on 25 March I was within 90 miles of Punta del Este in a 20 to 25 knot north-westerly, making good time within 10 degrees of the rhumb line. Would I make it?

After a terrific day's sailing the wind dropped altogether at dusk, having been sucked up into a huge line of black cloud that had been travelling to windward toward me all day. Now the massive line squall was vertically over me and *Newcastle Australia* rocked and rolled in the leftover choppy sea. This line of cloud had every appearance of a classic southerly buster, identical to the one that had passed me in Bass Strait, except that it was deathly black in color. I dropped the mainsail and furled the genoa, leaving only the storm jib, which I had been using as a staysail, set. It was upon me in no time with an instantaneous 180 degree change in wind direction. The wind was now from the south-east.

I thought I would be clobbered by the wind but the change came in at only 20 to 25 knots. I reset sail and proceeded on my course. However, the new wind was blowing against the north-west chop and soon kicked up uncomfortable, ferocious little waves of about 8 feet (2.4 m). We slammed into and dropped off one every few seconds and there was spray everywhere.

By now I was in regular radio contact with BOC control via the radio room at Punta del Este Yacht Club. I could see the loom of the lights of the resort city and set an estimated time of arrival, typically, for the wee hours the following morning.

I was able to sail reasonably fast on the new breeze but it showed signs of backing to the north-east, which would enable me to just lay my course. It was exciting closing land but I could not go down below and rest for a minute as I was constantly called to adjust the sail trim and steering oar due to the bumpy chop. I could not afford to lose any mileage by slipping off the breeze for comfort and speed and I knew I would find it very hard to beat back against the wind that was continually shifting further to the north. I did not care now, one more night and I could put up with anything, but it quickly became exhausting adjusting the steering oar for every wave.

Finally the lights of Punta del Este appeared clearly on the horizon and I had only 20 miles to sail. A few hours later, when within 10 miles, the wind let me down totally by suddenly going to the north, directly where I was going, and becoming light. I had to tack constantly with *Newcastle Australia* creeping sideways on each new heading. Neither tack was favorable. I knew that I would have to put up with this a bit longer.

Cindy, who along with many of the BOC officials and friends were waiting up for me, continued to party as I revised my arrival time yet again.

The northerly faded as I worked my way closer to land and I wondered if I was ever going to finish this leg. Tack, drift, tack, drift.

At about 0500 hours the lights of a motor launch came into view. I was delighted to hear that Cindy, Polly and Kat, two girls from the race office, were aboard to welcome me in. Also Billy Black, the renowned American marine photographer, had come out to capture the misery of a solo sailor in action.

It was great to call across the water to each other but this was one passage end for which I did not particularly feel like having witnesses. I was embarrassed to have kept everyone up all night, and by *Newcastle Australia*'s dishevelled appearance—dirty old sails, a mast with too much rake, and a weird tail-like device hanging off the back. Nothing like her former glory.

▲ *Crossing the line in Punta del Este. The condition of the boat and sails is obvious*   JANE McCONNELL

It was to be another 3 hours before I stumbled across the finish line. At about 0730 hours, with only a mile to go, the official BOC inflatable dinghy powered up alongside. I was making about 1 knot in the waning breeze. These people must be very patient. It was always a pleasure to see Mark Schrader in the official welcoming committee. Herb McCormick was there, as was Katie Ackland from Comsat, the provider of our wonderful satellite communication equipment. Cindy had transferred over to the inflatable dinghy and was, as usual, looking gorgeous, with a huge grin on her face.

▲ *Arriving in Punta del Este. Note the jury rudder*   JANE McCONNELL

I started to relax, deciding that if they could wait, I could too. As our little group drifted slowly toward the finish line off the breakwater I was further surprized and a little overwhelmed to see two more launches approach from the inner harbor. There were about thirty people on the boats, with David and Caroline Adams calling across greetings. Phil Lee, David's shore crew, was in a mood for celebrating. There were also several shore crews from the other boats on board. The shore crew of *Sceta Calberson* were buzzing around in a bright orange rigid inflatable dinghy. I could not believe the reception.

Like a soldier dragging his wounded self back from the front, at 0830 hours on 26 March *Newcastle Australia* grabbed a last puff of wind and slipped quietly over the line to the sound of a gun blast and horns from the motor boats. I had finally completed leg three of the BOC Challenge in fifty-six days 10 hours and 35 minutes (we will not worry about the seconds). *Newcastle Australia* and I were slightly scarred but, by the grace of God, had come through.

I had made it for Cindy's birthday and was delighted to help her on board for the tow into our berth. Mark and Herb were next on board, followed by David and Phil, who immediately set about furling sails and hooking up the tow. I was shoved aside and gladly handed over my charge to my more than competent helpers.

However, I was in for more surprizes as we rounded the breakwater. I could see a crowd of people on the dock as more than one hundred and fifty people had gathered to welcome me in. Most of the skippers and BOC entourage were there. It was incredible as we tied up to cheers and shouted well-wishes. When we finished securing *Newcastle Australia*, the whole group started singing 'Happy Birthday' to Cindy. It was an amazing experience.

CHAPTER TWELVE

Punta del Este: five days and a reprieve

DURING the week that I sailed *Newcastle Australia* without a rudder, David Adams and his shore crew, Phil Lee, had been working with Cindy to organize making a new one for me. They had been in touch with and received details from our designer, David Lyons, in Sydney and they had begun to source what materials were available in Punta del Este and Montevideo.

It was impossible to find enough polyvinyl chloride (PVC) foam core material to shape the rudder blade so it was decided to buy marine plywood and laminate and shape a new rudder blade from that. It would not be a perfect weight but it would be more than strong enough. A group of volunteers was quickly rounded up from among the fleet to help with the construction. The skippers of *Sceta Calberson* and *Hunters Child* provided much of what we needed from their stocks of repair materials. This included epoxy resin and enough carbon fiber and Kevlar fabrics to make a wonderfully strong yet light laminate.

To save time and maintain accuracy, it was logical to use the 2 foot (0.6 m) piece of rudder shaft that was left inside the boat between the bearings at hull and deck level. As I was being towed into the docks, Phil Lee began to dismantle my steering quadrant so that the surviving part of my rudder shaft could be extracted and used as the basis of the new shaft.

▶

Steve Pettingill from
Hunters Child *in Punta
del Este*

It would mean we would not have to rebuild the machined bearing surfaces. This would save much time and money and would also ensure that the new rudder fitted into the boat.

I could not believe the enthusiasm of everyone involved. I was told to clear off and have a rest. Phil took on the role of project manager and oversaw the entire operation as well as tending to the details of *True Blue*'s preparations.

I was physically burnt out after my passage from Sydney. Although we had so much help with the rudder I knew we would be hard pressed to get the boat ready in the five days that remained before the restart.

I had arrived on Sunday morning, 26 March, and the restart was scheduled for the following Saturday, 1 April. Cindy and I spent a quiet day together in celebration of her birthday. A casual dinner out at a restaurant was a welcome change from my unimaginative sailing diet—and the company was certainly better. The stress and fatigue of my passage began to slip into my memory.

Cindy and I discussed the possibility of flying my brother Mick over for the last few days to help work on the many other projects that needed doing before I could leave. As always we were stuck for cash. We made arrangements with Jayes in Newcastle, the agent we had booked all of Cindy's flights through. They had always been helpful and supportive when dealing with her erratic travelling schedule. They had no problem issuing Mick with tickets on the next flight, which we could pay for later.

The first stage of repairing the rudder was to rebuild the stainless steel shaft so that the blade could be built up around it. On Monday afternoon, Phil headed off to Montevideo, 60 miles away, to a machine shop to fabricate the new structural part but he did not return until the next day. It turned out that he had pressed the urgency of our situation on the three engineers who ran the business and kept them at their task for over 14 hours throughout the night. There was no stainless steel tube available so they had to roll and weld a stainless steel flat plate into a tube and machine it round. There was over 40 hours of labor in the original shaft and they completed the job in one session.

Enough plywood had also been located after an exhaustive search. On Tuesday, Merf Owen from *Thursday's Child*, with the help of Pete Robie, started to laminate the sheets together so they could be shaped into a perfect foil section. The epoxy resin had to cure under clamps overnight so the shaping began on Wednesday afternoon.

Mick arrived on the Wednesday morning and I was grateful that he had come at a moment's notice to lend a hand. In his cool, methodical way he zealously set to my job list without any fuss or bother.

While the shaping of the blade was being done in two halves, the next stage was to dig out a rebate from the solid blade, before it was epoxied and clamped together, so that the new shaft/stock would fit inside. The shaping went on late into the night, mostly by Merf, Pete and Dave Barnaby. Concurrently, another team had volunteered to chisel out the rebate. As one half of the shaping was finished, the rebating began.

As all of the BOC boats were of modern composite construction, the whole group had to search hard to find a few basic wood-working tools. There were about three small chisels available to rebate the hard plywood. The lack of proper hand or electric tools made this process very tedious. But where there is a will there is a way. Obviously, we could not all work at once so Phil delegated a time slot for each of the volunteers, who remained unflinching at the prospect of an all-night vigil, hammering away with the blunt and undersized chisels.

I was totally amazed to hear that David Scully of *Coyote* had put his hand up for the 0100 to 0500 time slot. And JJ Provoyeur of *Novell South*

Africa spent a couple of hours late that night helping out, dressed in his good club blazer. This was two nights before they would be at sea racing their own boats.

It must be remembered that the people who put so much effort into this were also busy working to prepare their own skippers' boats. It was amazing to be the recipient of so much good will. We had helpers at some stage from every boat in the fleet.

▲ *The rudder team: Billy Black, Dave Barnaby, Merf Owen, Skip Miller, Phil Lee and Mick Nebauer (left to right)*

Everyone worked on our repairs as if it were their own team's campaign. They were all skilled in their own fields and helped with as much enthusiasm and effort as if I was on the winning boat. Their attitude was not 'it'll do' but rather 'it must be done right'. My thanks extend to everyone involved, specifically Phil and Robyn Lee, David Adams, Pete Robie, Greg Smith, Merf Owen, Kate Ford, Skip Miller, Andy Darwent, Christian Brit, Dave Barnaby, Billy Black, Mick Nebauer, Anthony (*Novell*), Pablo, JJ Provoyeur, David Scully, Mark Schrader, Horatio, Steve Pettingill and the *Sceta Calberson* team.

The banging and grinding went on into the night and it was with cheers from a dozen workers when finally, at 0200 hours on Thursday morning, the rudder halves were spread with thick epoxy resin and glued and clamped together, permanently encapsulating the new rudder stock.

For all of Wednesday and Thursday, Christian Brit, the French composite expert from *Sceta Calberson*'s team, spent his time cramped under *Newcastle Australia*'s cockpit, grinding and then making an epoxy fiberglass repair to the rudder tube where it had cracked and leaked.

On Thursday the rudder was shaped further and then the whole assembly was transferred into the Yacht Club basement for the epoxy laminating to take place. Christian Brit took over now as glassing was his forte. After another night shift, not nearly as harsh as the previous one, our 'low-tech' timber and metal rudder took on a 'high-tech' skin of carbon and Kevlar cloth.

▲ *The rudder being laminated*

During all this I was in a bit of a daze, still dizzy with my transition back to shore life. I was not as productive as I knew I could be and was in awe of what was happening. I still had to help with work on board, which was coming along well. Kate Ford and Phil's wife, Robyn, were repairing some running rigging and stitching all the sail slides onto the mainsail I had got in the Falkland Islands, which had previously been connected with steel shackles that dangerously hooked up on things as the sail went up or down.

Before each leg restart every boat was scrutinized by BOC control to ensure it met safety requirements, and it was a priority that I was inspected and passed before the deadline. We found that I lacked a radar reflector as I had lost it when I lost the mast and it had been overlooked on our replacement gear list. Now we were struggling to find one. I was feeling stressed and gave Horatio, the friendly Uruguayan that was my scrutineer, a few headaches over this seemingly insignificant oversight. However, the rules had to be met.

The following day I was blessed. As a smiling Horatio boarded *Newcastle Australia* he presented me with a new, American-made radar reflector saying 'It is yours, it is a gift'.

Both David Adams and Giovanni Soldini offered me the use of their spare mainsails so that I would be more competitive for leg four. However, the sails had to be modified and with such tight time constraints this was impossible. Giovanni did lend me his spare blade headsail that I was able to recut and use with much more effect than the old rag I had been sent from England.

On Friday morning our rudder team eagerly arrived at the basement of the Yacht Club for a final fairing of the rudder and application of a coat of antifouling paint. I did not mind that the paint used was bright blue instead of *Newcastle Australia*'s usual black.

At 1600 hours that afternoon, while the boat was being buffeted by the strong wind and rain, my brand new 'miracle' rudder was pushed on a trolley down the dock to *Newcastle Australia*. Only a few people were needed to maneuver the trolley, however, a crowded escort was forming. Everyone was thrilled by the results of the team effort to build the rudder. I was speechless as we lifted the rudder and lowered it into the water with ropes. We had a diver in the water to position the shaft in the bottom bearing in the hull.

After a few moments in the murky water the diver was able to locate the shaft into the bearing and we were able to pull it through into the boat for alignment and final connection of the steering cables. Needless to say it fitted perfectly. I was overwhelmed with gratitude to Phil and all the willing helpers.

However, the restart was set for noon the following day and there still were many jobs to be done. Mick was busy installing a new radar and Cindy was reprovisioning. The gale was still blowing and rumors of a possible postponement to the start day were rife. The harbor had been closed now for two days because of rough weather. In my heart I was hoping that the start would be delayed as it looked as though I would not be ready to start

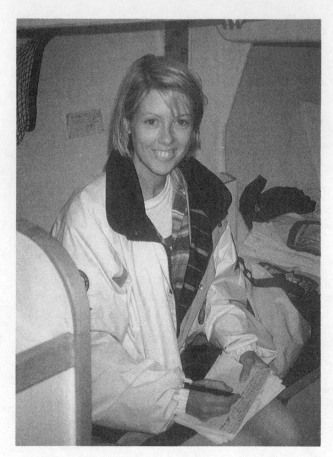

Cindy in Punta del Este writing one of the many lists

with the fleet. I was considering the possibility of leaving on the Saturday night when the jobs were done. I would miss the start by about 12 hours—time I could ill-afford.

That night was the prize-giving event for leg three. Distractedly Cindy and I went with the rest of the competitors to a glitzy hotel on the other side of town. I was not in a party mood, feeling under pressure from the imminent restart. I would have preferred to be in my room sorting charts and considering the next stage of my voyage.

It was a wild night outside with rain pouring and there was a southerly blowing at around 50 knots. The rough conditions were unsettling most of us as well as slowing down work on the boats when there was so little time left before the restart. However, it was a pleasant evening with much less razzamatazz than the event in Sydney. All competitors received a plaque for completing the leg as well as a traditional gold earring to commemorate our rounding of Cape Horn. The divisional placegetters also received their trophies. I nearly fell over when called forward to receive, for the second time, the leg trophy for 'outstanding seamanship' in recognition of rounding the Horn under jury rig and for later dealing with the loss of my rudder. In Cape Town I had received the same award for the rescue of Josh Hall. It was unprecented for one competitor to receive two such awards in the twelve-year history of the BOC Challenge. I was thrilled, of course, although surprized. However, I would much rather have sailed the leg with speed and obscurity.

Saturday morning dawned with no change to the furious conditions of the previous two days. The gale-force winds had torn the harbor up into a mass of broken water. The BOC officials were up at daylight to check the conditions and forecasts. As the harbor was still closed to traffic, it was decided that conditions were unsuitable for the restart. In fact, it would have been impossible to tow the competing boats away from the dock without severe damage occurring. There was too much risk so early on for a 6000 mile voyage.

I was elated with the news of my reprieve. A 24 hour delay meant I would be able to start with the rest of the fleet. Some of the skippers were disappointed at not being able to leave, having spent the previous night with the usual pre-start tension. But we all knew it was the right decision. For me it was a heaven-sent opportunity. I was still in the race. I did not have a chance against David or Giovanni but I was determined to arrive in Charleston in third place.

Mick was relieved that he had more time to finish the jobs. He had been so concerned that I would be leaving unprepared that he had opted to miss the prize-giving party and had stayed up late into the night finishing many things off. He was back on the boat from 0500 hours up the mast in the gale-force winds installing the new radar antenna he had brought with him from Australia.

During this extra day we tied up most of the loose ends and *Newcastle Australia* was again in operable condition. She was not perfect but at least now she would sail in a straight line. The mainsail was more organized and would set more efficiently. The jib from *Kodak* was almost new and, even though it did not fit properly, was strong and reliable. I spent some of this day finally sorting my charts and looking at the course options for leg four.

The best part, however, was spending those extra hours with Cindy. Knowing that the rudder was finished and that *Newcastle Australia* was as ready as we could make her, I was much more relaxed and started to look forward to the next stage of the voyage—a mere 6000 miles up to Charleston on my favorite ocean, the Atlantic. We knew we now would be able to finish what we had started so long ago. Cindy and I both felt blessed and humbled by all of the help we had received. Now it was time to go sailing.

CHAPTER THIRTEEN

Match race to Charleston

Six thousand nautical miles was all that remained of our race around the world. We had sailed over 21 000 miles since leaving Charleston only seven months earlier. On the one hand it seemed as though the event had been in progress forever; on the other it seemed like no time since the fleet had departed from South Carolina.

So far there had been more surprises for me than I had counted on. But with each difficulty I had positive experiences—from the generosity and enthusiasm of the people we had met, our sponsors and supporters and the helpers along the way, to the more personal lessons from which I was learning about life, my faith and, of course, sailing and seamanship.

At the start of leg four I was very keen to sail as hard and as fast as *Newcastle Australia* would let me. David Adams had spoken to me the day before the start when I was exhausted from trying to get everything done and also frustrated that my overall performance was not as good as I had wanted. He reaffirmed how important it was for me just to finish. It did not matter now that I would not be placed third overall but that I should sail well and conserve the boat. It was not worth risking the boat to prove a point. I only had to finish to achieve my goal.

So, at noon on Sunday, 2 April, as I was swapping tacks with David and the other competitors as we crossed the line for the last leg to Charleston,

▲ *A close race start at Punta del Este*   BILLY BLACK

I was not too worried about the other boats in the fleet, my objective for this leg being to beat my old mate Niah on *Jimroda II*. He was pleased with his standing so far, being overall third in Class II at this stage. I like Niah, but for this leg I was determined to be ruthless. I felt that this was my leg and that without any problems with the boat I could still sail faster than Niah. This was going to be a race between *Jimroda II* and *Newcastle Australia*.

There are two choices when sailing north from Uruguay. The first is to sail the more direct route close to shore and inside the south-setting Brazil current, in similar conditions to those on the east coast of Australia, making short tacks against the wind. The second is to sail further east before turning north, hoping to pick up the south-east trade winds that would send us swiftly to the equator and into the North Atlantic Ocean. Most of the fleet opted to sail further offshore, as did I. On the first night out, when we had started to spread out a little and the larger boats were over the horizon, I saw a sail several miles astern of me. I knew instantly that this was Niah.

We left Punta del Este in a fresh wind from the south-west but once we cleared the harbor we were in the lee of the land and heading north-east. The wind clocked round to the south and we made steady speed, reaching

▲ *With Niah Vaughan in port—on talking terms*   KATHERINE PAINE

in 15 knots with a rolly leftover swell from the recent storm. The wind was fluky in direction and later was back more from the west. I was quite nervous the first night out about nothing in particular—probably just tension, I guessed, from the hectic stopover. My week in Punta del Este had gone by quickly.

With Niah sailing so near it was exciting racing. I saw him the first night out until about 0100 hours, when his navigation lights disappeared from view. Where was he? Had he slipped by me? I was relieved in the morning to receive the fleet positions and to learn that he was safely astern of me. My work would be cut out to keep ahead of Niah but I was determined to regardless.

My first waypoint was more than a thousand miles up the coast, off Cabo Frio near Rio de Janeiro. I hoped to be securely in the south-east trades by the time I reached this area. However, the wind remained favorable only for the first 30 hours out of Punta del Este, clocking round until it blew from the north-east. As my course was roughly north-east, needless to say *Newcastle Australia* started to bash away to windward. It seemed that each tack was putting me further from my waypoint—but then that is sailing. I found that in light headwinds with my old undersized sails,

Newcastle Australia's performance was nowhere near what she was capable of. But at least I was able to carry on. I did not really care what winds I had as long as Niah had them too. I was worried that if he broke away from me and got into the north-east trades above the equator before me I would have no hope of catching him.

The Thursday after the start was my thirty-second birthday.

---

6 APRIL
My log reads:

Pretty dull old day ... celebrated with a Coke at tea time.

I was drifting in sight of Niah in very light winds. The sea was like a mirror. We played a match race, each of us tacking to cover the other, and we chatted for a while on VHF radio.

By the end of the first week the lead boats had broken into the trade winds and my log notes David Adams sailing fast in 15 to 20 knot easterlies. At this stage he had been further east of me and to my north. David, however, must have crossed a line of breeze, shutting the door behind him. Those left behind, which was most of the Class II boats and a couple of the older Class I boats, had to beat to windward for another 1000 miles before the breeze had any helpful east in it.

There were now two distinct groups, those who had favorable breeze and those who did not. I felt sorry for JJ Provoyeur, who had been sailing well in his older 60 foot (18.2 m) *Novell South Africa*, staying with the other Class I boats. He must have been right on the dividing line between the favorable and unfavorable breeze and found himself locked out as the lighter headwinds enveloped him and slowly moved north with him firmly in their grip.

Giovanni on *Kodak* was leading Class II but on 8 April reported a broken forestay. Everyone was amazed as he continued to manage very high average daily runs with the damaged rig. David Adams faxed headquarters:

▶ -- ◀
Should someone tell Giovanni that he has a damaged rig?
▶ -- ◀

Giovanni's plan was to divert to Vitória on the coast of Brazil, 300 miles to the north. He made arrangements to fly a new forestay out from Italy, hoping for a quick stopover. However, a few days later as he approached

Vitória he received word that his parts had missed the plane. What a blow to have diverted and lost ground to no avail.

However, with gritted teeth Giovanni continued on to Recife, a further 700 miles to his north. He must have had to keep his eye on the mast as he blasted off, finally reaching Recife and the vital components. He was able to get the repaired *Kodak* back out to sea in a matter of hours, only to find that the favorable breezes had abandoned him. He struggled north into the doldrums, losing ground every minute, while the lead boats sailed through without a murmur.

Meanwhile, I was still firmly locked in a tussle with *Jimroda II*.

1630 8 APRIL
My log reads:

It's amazing. Niah and I have been in VHF range for 1000 miles and in sight of each other for most of that time.

It was incredible how each day would see us leapfrog one another. In some conditions *Jimroda II* would stomp over *Newcastle Australia*, only a short time later to have a wind shift or strength change that would see *Newcastle Australia* stomp over *Jimroda II*. At one stage I lost sight of Niah, who also went firmly into 'stealth mode', not coming up on any radio schedules. I always knew, however, that he would be lurking in the background, listening to the radio in case I spoke to someone revealing my whereabouts. It was nerve-racking to make uninformed decisions in the hope that you could gain an advantage but also knowing that, with the boats separated, Niah could be in more favorable conditions.

I had been unable to sail as high as Niah as we neared Cabo Frio, mainly because of my inadequate sails and the severe lumpy chop we were bashing into. Thus I lost some ground to leeward. It was obvious that in these conditions he had better boat speed as he established a 40 mile lead. In a fax to headquarters, I noted that I was wearing my 'chasing *Jimroda* frown' again! I had to do something radical if I was to get back in front. Anticipating his moves for the next couple of days, and hoping the breeze would remain consistent, I headed off on a make or break track of my own.

It was disconcerting to lose touch with my rival. Niah had sailed north and west of me, while I started making short tacks to the north-east. It was important to keep a safe distance offshore, away from the many oil rigs that clutter the area east of Cabo Frio. The whole fleet seemed to have trouble near this area with headwinds forcing everyone down among the rig platforms, about 40 to 60 miles from the coast. It was tack, tack every 2 hours for two days with no word from *Jimroda II*. The silence was deafening and I was wondering what tricks Niah had up his sleeve and whether my decision would pay off.

The only feedback I could get as to our relative progress was the morning fleet position reports, but it seemed a long time between each of these. The winds remained from the northerly quarter and headed me on either tack. The sun shone out of a clear sky and the water temperature was warm. With conditions a far cry from those down south, I was content to be bashing away to windward in such fine weather.

One morning I was surprized to see a ship nearby, which appeared to be heading away from me. However, after some time it was apparent that I was gaining on it. As I drew closer I could see more detail. It was lying dead in the water, not moving, just drifting and looking abandoned. After repeated hails by radio to which I received no answer it soon disappeared astern of me as I continued on my course.

Shortly after this I sailed through a pod of pilot whales. They were mostly about 20 feet (6 m) long and there were several smaller, perhaps younger, ones among them. I had come on deck after hearing a squeaking sound similar to that of dolphins to see about fifteen of them cruising casually on either side of *Newcastle Australia*. My instinct was to dodge them but as they were ambling along on both my port and starboard sides I had nowhere to go. The group gave no impression of being nervous or of making any threatening moves as I sailed with them for a few minutes before they resumed their track to wherever.

The following afternoon the wind began to drop off quietly as some large black clouds started to develop to my east. By now I was at 20 degrees south and the lead boats to the north of me had complained of many frequent rain squalls while in this area, but they also were in good easterly breezes. Maybe we were nearing a zone of trade winds.

Plodding along in the waning breeze and unsure of exactly where my rival Niah was, I was constantly scanning the horizon, always watchful in case our paths should cross. At 1600 hours on 13 April I noted in my log that a sail was in sight several miles to my north-east. I was excited, of course, and moved silently about the deck as if any movement would give away my location.

The tracks of the two vessels were converging underneath huge anvil-topped thunderclouds. *Newcastle Australia* was heading on a port tack while the other boat was sailing in a north-westerly direction on a starboard tack. As we drew nearer I could positively identify the boat as *Jimroda II*. I was hoping Niah was asleep or otherwise distracted so that I could drop in on him unannounced. It was thrilling to be back in proximity of Niah. If we were near each other at least I could cover him until I could make a break into the fresher trade winds of the North Atlantic Ocean.

By now it was nearing dark and the huge clouds that were moving in on us, stealing the breeze, had taken on a sinister look. A black-purple mass was steadily moving over us. The wind-driven rain obliterated the horizon from my view as the squall line approached. I prepared the boat for the expected onslaught, reefing the mainsail and readying the jib for a quick douse if need be.

By now the two boats were separated by only a few hundred feet and the last thing I needed was for Niah to give me the slip under cover of the squall. With increasing speed the shadow of the clouds overtook *Newcastle Australia* and the day became as black as night. The wind, which had been from the north-east, flicked dramatically to the south, increasing in strength. The boat heeled sharply as the line of rain hit and we began to surge forward with the pressure. A few short minutes later, however, and the wind disappeared with a puff, leaving *Newcastle Australia* wallowing with slatting canvas. It was so quiet after the brief commotion that I could hear the sound of rainwater dripping off the sails onto the deck.

Newcastle Australia had been the first to get this change and we charged toward *Jimroda II*, narrowing the gap. As it was now time to report our positions to race headquarters it was amusing to hear *Newcastle Australia* and *Jimroda II* report identical positions. Our race was back on.

The wind remained fickle in the wake of the cloud bank and all through the night it clocked around the compass, varying in strength. Niah and I spoke on VHF radio as we sailed alongside each other, at times only a couple of boat lengths apart. *Jimroda II* was steering with a windvane self-steering device and I could see her lift up and knock down on the wind shifts. It was to be a long night, having to keep watch when in such close proximity to another vessel. However, the moon came out and *Jimroda II* looked magnificent, heeled to port with the light of the moon making her backlit sails appear translucent. I sat on deck admiring my comrade/rival's boat. I am sure that neither of us slept in our efforts to outsail each other. But in those conditions we were locked firmly together, sailing our parallel course.

The next morning *Jimroda II* was in sight, several miles astern. We were both now sailing in almost no wind, with rain and full cloud cover. It was a dismal day but I was happy to be in front of my antagonist, Niah. I found that in very light winds (less than 5 knots), even though *Newcastle Australia* was undercanvassed, I could slip along nicely with an advantage due to her light weight. However, in winds of 5 to 15 knots, *Jimroda II* had the advantage with a much more variable sail plan. So, naturally, I was hoping for fresh or zero winds—whatever it took to keep moving faster than Niah. Christophe on *Sceta Calberson* had already crossed the equator, sailing at 13 knots.

The constant effort involved in sailing so close to a rival was very draining. There was no opportunity to forget the race or even to read for half an hour to relax. It was trim, trim, and more trim, spinnaker up and spinnaker down.

The winds continued to remain unstable and doldrum-like, a situation I was not expecting until further north nearer the equator. However, the wind direction was at least favorable, tending to blow from the east and sometimes even a little south of east. However, it continued to blow very lightly as we progressed north along the Brazilian coast off Recife.

At one stage Niah, only 10 miles south of me, was in totally different winds. He had sailed all night under clouds that created fluky headwinds, causing him to tack half a dozen times; whereas I, fortunately, was just clear of the clouds in light winds that allowed me to sail a steady course all night without having to tack.

0800 15 APRIL
My log reads:

Rather him than me, I am just too tired.

During the evening on the fourteenth night of this leg I spoke to the officer on watch of an iron ore carrier, *The Equinox*, southbound from Newcastle, England.

The wind settled into the east and south-east for a few days, which was favorable and a relief after 1800 miles of windward sailing. However, it continued to remain very light, rarely blowing over 10 knots, until I was well north of the equator.

As we sailed closer to the equator, the winds became even more fickle with little squalls constantly on the horizon causing local disturbances. On 18 April I arrived at my second waypoint, off the north-east bulge of Brazil just north of Natal, and was able to turn the corner, heading onto an almost direct course towards Charleston. It was really satisfying to change course with just over 3300 miles remaining to the finish.

That same night I was flying a spinnaker and making good progress at the top of the range for that sail. I had been debating whether to take it down or to push on hard-pressed for a little longer. I knew I was taking miles off Niah. Suddenly the rope that was bracing the spinnaker pole back off the forestay parted with a soft bang and there was green and white nylon flogging and billowing out of control. This put an end to that debate as I rushed forward to douse the flapping sail before any damage could be done.

I made reasonable progress through the night only to lose the wind totally by morning. The equator was beginning to become very elusive and hard to reach. It was only 180 miles away but at only 1 or 2 knots it felt a million miles away. I lost sight of Niah the evening before as he had made a dash off to the west of my track. I could only guess at his position. Later that day, a fresh north-east breeze filled in after a huge squall passed. The wind built to about 20 to 30 knots, blasting me off on course averaging more than 10 knots. I imagined Niah being left astern as I sailed on in my own personal gale into the night.

The sky had become solid black, full of huge cumulus storm clouds. It was a little scary to be sailing at speed on such a night after days of pleasant sailing in sunshine. Overcoming the impulse to reef the sails, I pushed on fully powered with water ballast for the first time in days over the flat sea. It was incredible how quickly I forgot the drifting of the days before. It seemed as if this breeze was mine and would have me over the equator and in Charleston in no time. However, this was not to be. After 4 hours of brilliant speed the breeze began to fade and my boat speed dropped from averaging 10 to 11 knots to below 10 knots and then suddenly down to 4 to 5 knots. Sailing on through the remainder of the night I was content to believe that the wind had been put on just for me and that maybe Niah was languishing astern, more than 50 miles in my wake.

At around daylight or 0600 hours I went on deck after some sleep and began my ritualistic scan of the horizon. My binoculars were wearing out after months of use and the frequent lashings of salty spray and as I peered through the slightly misted lens I was taken aback to see a smudge on the horizon. Of course it was a sail and, by the look of it, was moving well in the light breeze on a course nearly parallel to mine.

My 'old mate' on *Jimroda II* had obviously been sailing in 'my' breeze last night. So much for exclusive wind shifts. I could see the familiar shape of *Jimroda II*'s sail plan becoming more distinct as Niah gradually overhauled me using his largest genoa to advantage. It was exasperating being unable to set any more sail. Several hours later *Jimroda II* was 50 feet (15.2 m) off my beam with Niah on deck grinning from ear to ear. Niah had raised an oversized British ensign and was flying it defiantly from the backstay. Shortly after the rogue Niah disappeared out of sight into a cloud bank.

◀

Jimroda II *sneaking past me*

Somehow during the night, however, we managed to swap positions again. The wind had dropped almost completely and *Newcastle Australia* slipped along with barely a ripple. The morning position report showed that Niah had dropped off to my west and I was in front for another turn.

The sky was continually overcast as neck and neck we approached the equator. Mostly it was very light wind with bursts of rain and squalls giving very little in the way of progress—it was fight for every mile. Once again *Newcastle Australia*'s light hull gave advantage as she would keep moving in the tiniest zephyr.

At 1500 hours local time on 21 April we had 18 miles to sail before crossing the equator. I was feeling great as I was in a patch of decent breeze for several hours as I worked my way closer to the North Atlantic Ocean, ticking away at between 8 and 9 knots. It always feels like a momentous occasion to change hemispheres but particularly this time as it really placed me on the home straight to Charleston.

The breeze stayed with me long enough to sneak across the equator at 1550 hours local time. I telephoned friends in England and America by way of celebration. Three hours after crossing into the Northern Hemisphere, however, *Newcastle Australia* was again drifting, only 6 miles north of the equator, as if we had all the time in the world. I spent that night making futile attempts to coax the boat along. The squalls only gave me rain with not a hint of wind.

At 0630 hours the following morning I was barely 28 miles north of the equator and on deck enacting my ritual (or was it becoming a nervous habit?) of scanning the horizon. I was dismayed to see that blasted British boat tearing up to me as *Newcastle Australia* sat motionless on the mirrored surface of the sea.

0630 22 APRIL
My log reads:

He's back!! Niah is about 3 miles astern of me and 3 to the east.

Even though I had crossed the equator more than 11 hours earlier than Niah he had sailed up on a new breeze. *Jimroda II* had carried the wind up to me (a good thing) but we did not benefit from the wind change until Niah was in sight of my position. Then it was on again in earnest.

Niah managed to give me the slip that day and increased his lead to about 25 miles over the next three days. This was really worrying for me as my main fear was that *Jimroda II* would pick up steady trade winds and shut me out. I ambled along in *Jimroda II*'s wake for the first few days after crossing over the equator, expectantly awaiting the promised trade winds.

On the evening of 23 April, three days into the North Atlantic Ocean, I was sailing in light winds with a spinnaker set. I was in the middle of speaking to Cindy on the AT&T radio telephone when I sensed a change in the boat's motion. Quickly disconnecting the call, I went on deck to discover a light mist rolling towards me from the north-east. The wind was steady from the east and we were moving nicely but the strange cloud, low to the surface, was unnerving. It was totally different to the usual equatorial squalls and I debated whether or not to drop the spinnaker.

I decided to follow my gut feeling and by the time I had lowered the huge green and white sail to the deck and stuffed half of it down the front hatch, the mist was swirling around my boat. As it did so the wind instantly switched to the north-east. The breeze filled in, at first gently, but gradually it increased to around 20 knots and settled in for the night.

With this amount of pressure on the beam, *Newcastle Australia* felt wonderful. I began to sail fast on the direct course to Charleston. This had to be the north-east trades. Suddenly, with the prospect of good boat speed again, Charleston began to seem not very far away. I pushed redial on my telephone handset and told Cindy that I was on the way.

I now began to make real progress toward the mark. After the first 24 hours of consistent breeze, which gave me a run of 238 miles, I felt it would be safe to say the north-east trades had established themselves. What a difference it made to be sailing fast. I had Niah in my sights and began to look forward to catching up to him again.

The following day I tuned in and listened to the chat hour. I had given up speaking on the radio several days before because I had decided I was giving too much away to the competition. I made a resolution not to speak on the chat hour but to concentrate more on sailing. At the end of the schedule I heard Niah call me on VHF radio. Ignoring him, I went on deck and to my delight I could see him off to starboard about 3 miles away. I had pulled him back a day sooner than expected—this was tremendous.

1600 26 APRIL
My log reads:

How wonderful to be sailing well. We have averaged 10 knots for the last couple of days—so the old girl still has it. Praise God. We have been in steady 18 to 21 knots for over 70 hours. It is amazing. Two mornings ago I was 25 behind Ni. Now I have 20 on him. All is well at home. Cindy is very busy with fundraising and getting ready to come to USA. She has been doing a wonderful job. I am looking forward to living with her and the kids again—being a family will be neat!! This morning Christophe had 248 miles to go so he should get in tomorrow. I have 2150 to go!!! Will look forward to next time—with lessons learnt.

Niah Vaughan and *Jimroda II* made a brilliant team throughout the whole race. His boat was much older and heavier than *Newcastle Australia* but Niah's determination and consistent efforts meant he drove his boat at her limits.

During the previous couple of days word had filtered in from home that David on *True Blue* had been having problems on board. He was leading Giovanni on *Kodak* by well over 400 miles and, overall, actually was in fifth position in the fleet. Typically, he had been very quiet about reporting any technical problems. I had noticed his course veering suspiciously west off the rhumb line but it was not until he was at sea again that I heard that he had called into the Caribbean Island of Antigua to repair his generator. Apparently the engine succumbed to some contaminated diesel fuel and had been causing trouble for several days. With reduced efficiency he faced the risk of total power loss for the critical final 1000 miles to Charleston.

David had telephoned his wife Caroline, requesting that their shore crew Phil Lee meet him in Antigua to help sort out the problem. David had been hand-steering 12 hours a day to conserve power before being forced to divert. Arriving in Antigua on the Monday morning, he was out again that same evening after a 9 hour stopover. Phil and David had been unable to repair the generator. So, unfazed, Phil went off and bought an old secondhand petrol-driven portable generator. Lashing the generator on deck in the cockpit, with jugs of the volatile fuel, David headed back out to sea and resumed racing. The improvised charging system lacked finesse but it was adequate for the remaining days of the race. Meanwhile, due to the diversion and delays, Giovanni had continued his relentless attack on the number one spot by taking almost 200 miles off David's lead.

It was interesting to realize that now, after David had been forced to seek port for repairs, each of the Class II boats except for the plucky Vaughan on *Jimroda II* had made an unscheduled stop during the race. Although Niah had considered calling into the Falkland Islands after a severe beating encountered after he passed Cape Horn, he had managed to keep things going until Punta del Este. The fatalities among the fleet, including the Class I boats, revealed just how serious a test this type of high-pressure voyaging is on yacht and crew.

At this stage, Charleston was preparing for the expected arrival of Christophe aboard *Sceta Calberson*. On the morning of 27 April, Christophe crossed the line to claim victory for his second successive BOC Challenge. He had won the 1990–91 race by 21 hours. This time his nearest rivals were a group of three Class I boats comprising Jean Luc Van den Heede, David Scully and Steve Pettingill, who were battling it out only miles apart for second place with over 600 miles still to go.

▲ *Christophe Auguin—twice winner of the BOC Challenge (1990–91, 1994–95)* BILLY BLACK/BOC

▲ Sceta Calberson   BILLY BLACK/ BOC

It was exciting watching the close of the race from an observer's viewpoint via satellite, while at the same time being intimately involved as a competitor. Christophe attributed his success not only to his ability on the water but also to his team, comprising designers and shore crew, having made the most of the year and a half of lead time they had for preparation. Even so, he experienced frustrations during leg one that put him further back in the field than expected, and he had done a brilliant job to pull back for an overall victory.

For me at sea it really brought home the fact that this incredible (?) experience was drawing to a close. I would have my hands full defending my position against Niah. Christophe's job was satisfactorily over but I still had work to do.

After five fantastic days of sailing in the north-east trades, covering more than 200 miles each day, my wind slowly began to get lighter and lighter. I had established a lead of 90 miles over Niah, who had several days earlier declared a radio silence—I liked to think this was brought on by the pressure of my lead. But he too was having generator problems. When he later had to shut down his Standard-C, it was a worry not being able to keep track of him from the daily position reports. With no idea of his position I could only sail my course trusting that he had no cards left to deal.

Three days after Christophe's decisive victory the group of three roared into Charleston led by Steve Pettingill, who was declared 'America's best', claiming second place overall. Steve achieved the highest ever placing for an American in the BOC Challenge. Six hours later David Scully arrived with Jean Luc Van den Heede, who was third overall, hot on his heels, separated by only 45 minutes. What an amazingly close race after 6000 miles. The trio had been separated by only a few miles for much of the last week, certainly making a sensational finish to their individual efforts.

The next day, 2 May, David Adams finished. He was expected to arrive around 0700 hours but his blazing dash to claim first place in Class II was stifled as when only 10 miles off Charleston the wind died, causing him to spend several hours surrounded by spectator boats as *True Blue* drifted across the line nearer to noon—a casual end to David's well-planned and well-executed victory.

David's record-breaking circumnavigation was a testimony to his forethought and planning, based on experience gained from his previous BOC Challenge. It was also an achievement for Australian sailing technology. David claimed the world record for 50 foot (15.2 m) boats and also the fastest circumnavigation ever by an Australian. Later he would be declared 1995 Australian Yachtsman of the Year. He was placed fifth overall, beating several Class I boats. I sent David a fax:

Up the Aussies.

Next to arrive was JJ Provoyeur with *Novell South Africa,* shaving almost a week off his boat's previous time around the course under the command of Bertie Reed during the 1990–91 BOC Challenge. Giovanni arrived next, a day or so later, for second place in Class II. Suddenly there was a hush after the excitement of half the fleet's arrival in Charleston. I found myself at the head of those remaining at sea, still with almost 900 miles to finish.

By now I was sailing over the top of the Caribbean Islands and working on the Atlantic chart, which showed my destination. There was a marked increase in the amount of vessels moving about. I frequently saw both commercial ships and private sailing boats. One evening I was belting along,

▲ *David Adams*   BILLY BLACK/BOC

▲ True Blue   BILLY BLACK/BOC

overpowered with the spinnaker up. While dumping the sail I noticed another sail on the horizon. Intrigued, I changed course slightly to sail a bit closer to the vessel. It turned out to be the 36 foot (11 m) *Flor* out of England with solo sailor, Dave Felthouse, aboard en route from the Canary Islands to Saint Lucia in the Caribbean. We chatted briefly on VHF radio and then went our separate ways.

As I neared the area north-east of Puerto Rico a couple of days later I could hear much traffic on the VHF radio. It turned out to be US naval planes patrolling a zone designated as a military target area. I could hear the planes hailing yachts and redirecting vessel traffic around the prohibited area. Apparently there was a joint forces exercise in progress. I was able to carry on my course, only clearing the area shortly before it was closed off. I was racing and terrified that they would tell me to alter course. I would have rather mixed it with a warhead than alter course at this stage of the race.

An interesting thing occurred as I tried to place a direct dial radio call to Josh Hall at race headquarters. The radio works on a duplex frequency whereby I transmit on one frequency and receive on another. As I activated the send button on the handpiece I heard the familiar chirping sound that indicated the call was ringing the desired number. I heard Josh's voice boom in as he answered. I responded with a greeting, only to hear Josh carry on speaking as if he had not heard me. Naturally I had assumed he had answered my call only to realize that Josh had two parties transmitting on the one frequency. I could only hear Josh but it turned out that Robin on *Cornwall* had dialled the same number seconds before me and it was his call that Josh had answered.

The wind had gone very light again and my daily runs were down to 130 miles, 83 miles and 110 miles. One day it was as low as 60 miles. I still had my lead over Niah and was determined to maintain it. From information gleaned by listening to the chat hour I noted that Niah and Arnie had opted to sail more directly toward Charleston. I had continued on my course, staying more to the left or western side of the course. For a while it appeared that they might overtake me as I struggled in light winds. *Jimroda II*'s position climbed to within 7 miles of my distance to go and it was looking pretty grim before a forecasted high pressure system developed, shutting Niah and Arnie out with fickle breezes and calms.

▲ *A quiet moment as I near Charleston*

Newcastle Australia was placed further south and west of the rhumb line and I found a favorable north-easterly breeze spinning off the bottom of the clockwise rotating system. This time it really seemed as though the wind was put on just for me. It continued to be favorable by clocking first east and then south, finally swinging and settling from the south-west as a new front moved across.

This new wind was incredible. I was almost in sight of Charleston with less than a few hundred miles left to go. *Newcastle Australia* finally had a bone in her teeth. With the spinnaker up and drawing the miles seemed to roll on by at an average speed of between 9 and 10 knots. The breeze as it veered into the south-west increased in strength and the boat was flying at speeds often up around 14 to 15 knots. I pushed the boat until the wind was up around 30 knots and it just became too dangerous to carry on with the spinnaker. For this whole leg I had been battling with the worry of another broken mast but now so close to home I had pushed on, almost beyond prudence.

Having left the spinnaker up for too long, I had to struggle for some time to then bring it down. Finally, with the burden of too much sail gone, the boat became almost sedate as she carried on at 11 knots with the mainsail and jib set. I had 222 miles to finish.

Cindy and the children were now in Charleston. They and my parents were staying at the home of the Hernandez family in Mount Pleasant, the city across the river from Charleston. Pepe and Cyndy Hernandez and their son Jose had befriended us prior to the race start in September. During the race they had been in touch with my family and offered them to stay after the race was over. It was wonderful to be the recipient of such hospitality and I was able to dial a local number on my radio handset to touch base with everyone.

It was always a relief to speak to Cindy after her long flight from Australia because we always lost a couple of days of contact while she was in transit. On her arrival day I was perhaps too keen to speak and called while she was sound asleep with jet lag. However, everyone there was keen to speak and it added to the sense of building climax knowing that my family was in town. I was heading to be with them, which was a much more exciting idea than merely heading to a foreign port.

If this pace kept up I would soon be in. Earlier in the week I had given a tentative estimated time of arrival of Friday. Now with the increased speed this was rapidly changing. It looked as though I would arrive on the next day, which was Thursday, 11 May. I was encouraged to think that, for once, I would not be keeping everyone awake with a late night landfall.

I was now sailing firmly in the Gulf Stream, the strong current that flows north up the east coast of America and eventually across the Atlantic Ocean toward Europe. With the fresh breeze the sea had become choppy even though the wind and current were favorable. I was passing through areas of strong eddies where the current would be against the wind, causing the seas to kick up uncomfortably. I was being drenched with spray for the first time in ages as *Newcastle Australia* leaped off wave after wave.

Late in the afternoon I was screaming along, exhilarated to be sailing so well with the end in sight—I had just on 200 miles to go. Suddenly I was shocked to hear a thump under the hull and I saw a baulk of timber roll out from under the boat. It was deja vu—almost a repeat of my collision with the Cuban raft on the first day of the race back in September. The timber floated away and I was relieved to see that it was nowhere near the size of the raft.

However, after a while I noticed my boat speed was down and that *Newcastle Australia* was cutting a disturbed wake. I peered over the side and once again experienced deja vu. A piece of board was hanging from the rudder. I slowed the boat down and, after about half an hour of hanging over the side, in and out of the water as the boat rolled, I was able to dislodge it by prodding it with a sail batten. I was relieved to get moving again. It seemed ironic that on the first and last days of this race I should have an incident with Gulf Stream flotsam. Was there a message here?

Back on track again I carried on averaging 10.3 knots. It was an amazing night as if the sea were reminding me to remain vigilant. The breeze never let up and actually began to veer more to the west. It was obvious that within not too many hours the wind would be strong from the north-west, right on the nose. I anticipated that I would be able to make it in just before the change and I held my course high, moving more to the west closer to the coast so that I could then swing my course around with the shift and maintain more of a favorable reaching angle for a longer period as I neared my goal.

I did not sleep that night. Every hour I would note my position to keep the boat as close to my course as possible, not giving any room for the current to set me north as this would make it difficult on my final approach. My log notes the rapid closure with an hourly adjusted distance to finish. Soon I had less than 100 miles to go. At 0500 hours on Thursday, 11 May, I had 91 miles to go. By 0600 hours I only had 76 miles to go—surely the Gulf Stream helped with that one.

When I was down to 50 miles to go I phoned Mick in Australia. It was late at night for him and after the call he did not sleep a wink all night. He was ecstatic and thanked me for letting him be involved. It was incredible. I had so much to be grateful for. By the grace of God I had come full circle. There were so many people to thank.

Later I rang Cindy to say I had 40 miles to go. Everyone at Pepe and Cyndy's were excited. Mum, Dad, Annie and Vance would be offshore to meet me on Pepe's motor boat, *Salsa*. Cindy would wait and meet me on the committee boat as usual with Mark and Herb.

Newcastle Australia seemed unstoppable and really took off once clear of the Gulf Stream and in the flatter water nearer to shore. At noon I was in sight of *Salsa*, which was rolling in the swell. I could barely see the flat Carolina coast from a few miles away although towers on shore could be seen for a position check to confirm the GPS position. I was in radio communication with Mark Schrader on the committee boat who told me to 'just follow us across the line'.

Thursday's Child was at least 90 miles behind and with no word from the incommunicado *Jimroda II* I could only imagine that he was somewhere near Arnie. I had beaten my noble adversary Niah for this last leg, which was very satisfying. However, the overall results would grant me fourth place as my accumulated problems added weeks to my time. Niah had beaten me after all with his consistent and stalwart *Jimroda II*.

Newcastle Australia flew in, close-reaching with the GPS reading 13 plus knots speed over the ground. It seemed as though she wanted to vindicate herself in public. I stood at the bow watching the last stages unfold as I barely had to adjust the autopilot as I neared the finish line. There were several motor boats and a couple of yachts out on the blustery day to see me in. *Salsa* had come out the furthest and was motoring off my beam, providing a welcome escort. There were about twenty people on board, all waving. I could see Dad holding onto a rail, looking solemn, just watching. Annie and Vance were sound asleep.

At 1421 hours local time, *Newcastle Australia* took the gun for an official finish of the 1994–95 BOC Challenge. Within a few minutes Cindy, Mark and Herb were on board, all soaking wet after hours in the high-speed inflatable dinghy. Phil Lee and Marko from *Sceta Calberson*'s team jumped aboard and took over the tow arrangements. John Griffiths, a friend from home, climbed across. There were handshakes all round. I grabbed Cindy in a big hug. We had made it. Fielding a barrage of questions from Herb, I was content to sit aft with Cindy, relinquishing command for the last time by letting Mark steer. Charleston Harbor looked fantastic.

▲ *Arrival in Charleston*   JOYCE TICKEL

Epilogue

——————

I HAD left Charleston almost eight months before and was here again, with the race completed, seeing it for the first time. Due to the frantic pre-race preparations, with ten days full of race briefings and official functions, my memories of Charleston were only of kind faces. I had had little time to see any of the surrounding area or to get to know the people. Now, with the race behind me, much of the pressure was off and I was free to spend time with my family and to get to know our new friends at a much more leisurely pace.

The race committee could not have found a better venue than Charleston for the start and finish of the BOC Challenge. Charleston was a fantastic experience in itself. The city center is quite old yet well maintained and much of the architecture dates from the eighteenth century. It has kept its unique character and charm with modern buildings being thoughtfully designed to blend with the old. It also offers a fine harbor. Situated on a peninsula, bordered by the Cooper and Ashley Rivers, everything is close at hand and the flat terrain lends itself to walking, which I think adds to the casual pace of life. In many ways it bears much similarity to the city of Newcastle in that it is a major port and has played a significant role historically in its country's early economic and strategic development.

The city was alive with enthusiasm for the BOC Challenge and each of the skippers was treated royally, irrespective of his place in the fleet. During the circumnavigation each of the skippers had been looking forward to returning to Charleston and we were all shown the epitome of true Southern hospitality. This Southern hospitality culminated at the final prize-giving ceremony some ten days after my arrival. Several thousand people turned out, filling the sporting complex used for the event. As with all other stopover ceremonies, we skippers became part of an exaggerated spectacle as images of our boats and faces were projected onto a huge screen. Words of congratulations were extended and each skipper was called forward in turn to receive his prize—we all received a trophy as a momento of our circumnavigation. Christophe Auguin was presented with the overall prize trophy and cheque for his second consecutive victory, first overall and in Class I. David Adams was awarded overall first in Class II—he had broken all previous Australian and 50 foot (15.2 m) yacht records.

For me, even though my overall position was fourth in Class II, my third place for leg four felt like a real victory. And again I was surprised to be presented with the IBM Performance trophy for exceptional seamanship overall in Class II.

I had now joined a small club, not only of those internationally who have completed the BOC Challenge, but also by becoming the sixth Australian to race solo around the world. It was a great privilege to follow in the wake of my fellow compatriots Neville Gossen (1982–83), Ian Kiernan (1985–86), Don McIntyre (1990–91), Kanga Birtles (1990–91) and David Adams (1990–91 and 1994–95). For me the race was everything I had expected and more. I look forward to the possibility of taking up the challenge again.

Overall results for the 1994–95 BOC Challenge

Competitors	Elapsed time day/hr/min/sec	Overall placing	Leg one placing	Leg two placing	Leg three placing	Leg four placing
Class I: 50–60 feet (15.2–18.2 m)						
Christophe Auguin (France)						
Sceta Calberson	121/17/11/46	1	3	1	1	1
Steve Pettingill (USA)						
Hunters Child	128/04/03/09	2	2	3	2	2
Jean Luc Van den Heede (France)						
Vendée Enterprises	129/17/59/38	3	4	2	3	4
David Scully (USA)						
Coyote	133/00/56/35	4	6	4	5	3
JJ Provoyeur (South Africa)						
Novell South Africa (Ben Vio)	133/05/11/41	5	5	5	4	5
Arnie Taylor (USA)						
Thursday's Child	200/01/45/26	6	7	6	6	6
Isabelle Autissier (France)						
Ecureuil Poitou Charentes 2	Leg one 35/08/52/18	DNF	1	Yacht lost		
Josh Hall (UK)						
Gartmore Investment Managers		DNF	Yacht sunk			
Mark Gatehouse (UK)						
Queen Anne's Battery		DNF	Retired			
Class II: 40–50 feet (12.2–15.2 m)						
David Adams (Australia)						
True Blue	131/05/06/39	1	1	1	2	1
Giovanni Soldini (Italy)						
Kodak	134/00/46/40	2	2	2	1	2
Chaniah Vaughan (UK)						
Jimroda II	166/16/06/13	3	3	4	3	4
Alan Nebauer (Australia)						
Newcastle Australia	181/13/46/28	4	4	3	4	3
Robin Davie (UK)						
Cornwall	197/04/15/28	5	6	5	5	5
Minoru Saito (Japan)						
Shuten-Dohji II	223/10/10/53	6	7	8	6	6
Floyd Romack (USA)						
Cardiac 88		DNF	11	Did not start		
Neal Petersen (South Africa)						
Protect Our Sea Life		DNF	9	Dismasted		
Simone Bianchetti (Italy)						
Town of Cervia, Adriatic Sea		DNF	8	Retired		
Nigel Rowe (UK)						
Skycatcher		DNF	5	6	Retired	
Harry Mitchell (UK)						
Henry Hornblower		DNF	10	7	Lost at sea	

Glossary

back The wind is said to back when it changes direction anticlockwise; for example, east to north-east.

backwinded A sail is backwinded when the wind blows on its lee side (the side opposite to that for which it is trimmed).

battens Lengths of fiberglass or other material fitted into pockets of a sail used to affect the shape of a sail.

chainplate Metal or reinforced fiber fitting at deck level to which is attached a yacht's standing rigging.

close-hauled A vessel is said to be close-hauled when the sails are trimmed close to the center line for a work to windward (*see* tack).

foil/fairing Terms used to describe the sectional shape of a modern yacht's fin keel.

galley Cooking area on a boat.

genoa A large triangular sail that is set forward of the mast and used in lighter winds.

God All references to God relate to the Lord Jesus Christ as outlined in the Bible.

gooseneck Fitting joining the boom to the mast, allowing movement vertically and sideways.

GPS Global Positioning System. Electronic navigation system using satellites to indicate a vessel's position—both latitude and longitude.

great circle route The shortest distance between two points on the earth's surface.

gybe To turn a sailing vessel so that the wind passes from one side to the other across the stern.

halyard Rope (Spectra or Kevlar) or wire used to raise and lower sails.

heave to To stop or nearly stop a vessel's headway with small opposing sails.

jib The foremost headsail. It can be a genoa jib or a blade jib.

jury rig A makeshift or substitute rig as may be arranged when masts or gear have been carried away.

keel box Stainless steel structural member used on *Newcastle Australia* to locate the keel into the hull.

Kevlar Modern fabric used instead of fiberglass as reinforcement in a boat's structure. The fibers are also used to make very strong light rope and sails offering minimum stretch or elasticity.

knockdown Term used to describe a vessel being layed flat by breaking seas such that the mast is in the water or below the horizontal.

knot A measure of speed. One knot equals one nautical mile per hour.

leech The aftermost edge of a sail.

Lexan Strong acrylic material used in hatches and windows of boats. It is usually transparent, clear or color-tinted.

luff The leading edge of a sail.

match race Competition between equal or nearly equal vessels where tactics play a major role as opposed to sheer boat speed determining the winner.

nautical mile An international unit of distance for sea and air navigation equal to 6076.115 feet (1852 m).

reaching Point of sail when the wind is blowing over a vessel's side beam.

reef To reduce the size of a sail by tying or rolling up a portion of the area to suit varying conditions (slab or roller furling).

rhumb line A straight line between two points on a nautical chart. Due to the earth's curvature it is not the shortest distance.

Spectra Synthetic fiber used in the manufacture of modern rope and sail fabrics.

spreaders Metal struts attached to the mast over which rigging is led to help support the mast sideways and to reduce compression loads.

Standard-C Data transfer satellite communciation system developed by Comsat.

tack 1. The lower and foremost corner of a sail where it is attached to the deck or mast fitting. 2. To beat or work to windward in a zigzag manner, close-hauled first on one tack and then on another. 3. Direction or course of a yacht in relation to the position of her sails. A yacht is on a starboard tack when the wind is on the starboard side.

veer The wind is said to veer when it changes direction clockwise; for example, east to south-east.

waypoint A position on a chart used as a destination or portion of a composite course. With a route from points A to B to C, point B would be the first waypoint in the route.

zulu Term used for GMT (Greenwich mean time) or UTC (univeral co-ordinated time). International standard of time relevant to Greenwich in England.

Route of *Newcastle Australia* in the 1994–95 BOC Challenge

Charleston (Race start: 17 Sep. 1994;
Race finish: 11 May 1995)

leg one

rescued Josh

leg
four

Punta del Este
(Arrived: 26 Mar. 1995;
Restart: 2 Apr. 1995)

knockdown
injury

leg three

Harry lost

dismasted

lost rudder

Falkland Islands

Cape Horn